CAREER EXAMINATION SERIES

C-3005

THIS IS YOUR **PASSBOOK®** FOR ...

NUTRITIONIST II

NATIONAL LEARNING CORPORATION®
passbooks.com

COPYRIGHT NOTICE

This book is SOLELY intended for, is sold ONLY to, and its use is RESTRICTED to individual, bona fide applicants or candidates who qualify by virtue of having seriously filed applications for appropriate license, certificate, professional and/or promotional advancement, higher school matriculation, scholarship, or other legitimate requirements of educational and/or governmental authorities.

This book is NOT intended for use, class instruction, tutoring, training, duplication, copying, reprinting, excerption, or adaptation, etc., by:

1) Other publishers
2) Proprietors and/or Instructors of «Coaching» and/or Preparatory Courses
3) Personnel and/or Training Divisions of commercial, industrial, and governmental organizations
4) Schools, colleges, or universities and/or their departments and staffs, including teachers and other personnel
5) Testing Agencies or Bureaus
6) Study groups which seek by the purchase of a single volume to copy and/or duplicate and/or adapt this material for use by the group as a whole without having purchased individual volumes for each of the members of the group
7) Et al.

Such persons would be in violation of appropriate Federal and State statutes.

PROVISION OF LICENSING AGREEMENTS. — Recognized educational, commercial, industrial, and governmental institutions and organizations, and others legitimately engaged in educational pursuits, including training, testing, and measurement activities, may address request for a licensing agreement to the copyright owners, who will determine whether, and under what conditions, including fees and charges, the materials in this book may be used them. In other words, a licensing facility exists for the legitimate use of the material in this book on other than an individual basis. However, it is asseverated and affirmed here that the material in this book CANNOT be used without the receipt of the express permission of such a licensing agreement from the Publishers. Inquiries re licensing should be addressed to the company, attention rights and permissions department.

All rights reserved, including the right of reproduction in whole or in part, in any form or by any means, electronic or mechanical, including photocopying, recording, or by any information storage and retrieval system, without permission in writing from the Publisher.

Copyright © 2018 by

National Learning Corporation

212 Michael Drive, Syosset, NY 11791
(516) 921-8888 • www.passbooks.com
E-mail: info@passbooks.com

PUBLISHED IN THE UNITED STATES OF AMERICA

PASSBOOK® SERIES

THE *PASSBOOK® SERIES* has been created to prepare applicants and candidates for the ultimate academic battlefield – the examination room.

At some time in our lives, each and every one of us may be required to take an examination – for validation, matriculation, admission, qualification, registration, certification, or licensure.

Based on the assumption that every applicant or candidate has met the basic formal educational standards, has taken the required number of courses, and read the necessary texts, the *PASSBOOK® SERIES* furnishes the one special preparation which may assure passing with confidence, instead of failing with insecurity. Examination questions – together with answers – are furnished as the basic vehicle for study so that the mysteries of the examination and its compounding difficulties may be eliminated or diminished by a sure method.

This book is meant to help you pass your examination provided that you qualify and are serious in your objective.

The entire field is reviewed through the huge store of content information which is succinctly presented through a provocative and challenging approach – the question-and-answer method.

A climate of success is established by furnishing the correct answers at the end of each test.

You soon learn to recognize types of questions, forms of questions, and patterns of questioning. You may even begin to anticipate expected outcomes.

You perceive that many questions are repeated or adapted so that you can gain acute insights, which may enable you to score many sure points.

You learn how to confront new questions, or types of questions, and to attack them confidently and work out the correct answers.

You note objectives and emphases, and recognize pitfalls and dangers, so that you may make positive educational adjustments.

Moreover, you are kept fully informed in relation to new concepts, methods, practices, and directions in the field.

You discover that you arre actually taking the examination all the time: you are preparing for the examination by "taking" an examination, not by reading extraneous and/or supererogatory textbooks.

In short, this PASSBOOK®, used directedly, should be an important factor in helping you to pass your test.

NUTRITIONIST II

DUTIES

Plans, develops, and directs the nutrition services program. Provides consultation and technical assistance to community agencies, health professionals, and the general public. Plans and conducts in-service education programs for professional staff. Develops and prepares educational articles or material, and evaluates information from other sources and promotes their utilization. Conducts studies and surveys to determine the need for nutrition services. Directs fieldwork of professional personnel. Does related work as required.

SCOPE OF EXAMINATION:

The written test will be designed to cover knowledges, skills, and/or abilities in the following areas:

1. **Basic nutrition and dietetics** - These questions test for knowledge of basic nutrition and dietetics. Topics may include the nutritional value of foods, nutritional needs of the persons served, balanced diets and specific foods and their relation to health.
2. **Patient/client dietary care** - These questions test for: knowledge of the relationship of nutrient intake to health and to restorative and rehabilitative medical treatment. Topics may include the selection of foods in accordance with a person's preferences, history and medical condition; foods included/excluded in commonly used special diets; and providing counseling and education about nutritional needs.
3. **Advanced nutrition and dietetics** - These questions test for an advanced knowledge of nutrition and dietetics. Topics may include the assessment of nutritional needs, nutritional care planning and the provision of therapeutic diets.
4. **Preparing written material** - These questions are designed to test how well you can express yourself in writing. Particular emphasis will be placed upon two major aspects of written communication: how to clearly and accurately express given information and how to present written material in the most logical and comprehensible manner.
5. **Providing services to women, infants and children** - These questions test for a knowledge of the special needs of the WIC program service population. Topics may include maternal and pediatric nutrition and common nutritional problems of the economically disadvantaged.
6. **Development, conduct and evaluation of training programs** - This subtest is designed to measure the candidate's ability to design, implement and evaluate training programs, including but not limited to such topics as assessment of training needs; selection of training materials and methods; teaching techniques; and handling of problem situations.

HOW TO TAKE A TEST

I. YOU MUST PASS AN EXAMINATION

A. WHAT EVERY CANDIDATE SHOULD KNOW
Examination applicants often ask us for help in preparing for the written test. What can I study in advance? What kinds of questions will be asked? How will the test be given? How will the papers be graded?

As an applicant for a civil service examination, you may be wondering about some of these things. Our purpose here is to suggest effective methods of advance study and to describe civil service examinations.

Your chances for success on this examination can be increased if you know how to prepare. Those "pre-examination jitters" can be reduced if you know what to expect. You can even experience an adventure in good citizenship if you know why civil service exams are given.

B. WHY ARE CIVIL SERVICE EXAMINATIONS GIVEN?
Civil service examinations are important to you in two ways. As a citizen, you want public jobs filled by employees who know how to do their work. As a job seeker, you want a fair chance to compete for that job on an equal footing with other candidates. The best-known means of accomplishing this two-fold goal is the competitive examination.

Exams are widely publicized throughout the nation. They may be administered for jobs in federal, state, city, municipal, town or village governments or agencies.

Any citizen may apply, with some limitations, such as the age or residence of applicants. Your experience and education may be reviewed to see whether you meet the requirements for the particular examination. When these requirements exist, they are reasonable and applied consistently to all applicants. Thus, a competitive examination may cause you some uneasiness now, but it is your privilege and safeguard.

C. HOW ARE CIVIL SERVICE EXAMS DEVELOPED?
Examinations are carefully written by trained technicians who are specialists in the field known as "psychological measurement," in consultation with recognized authorities in the field of work that the test will cover. These experts recommend the subject matter areas or skills to be tested; only those knowledges or skills important to your success on the job are included. The most reliable books and source materials available are used as references. Together, the experts and technicians judge the difficulty level of the questions.

Test technicians know how to phrase questions so that the problem is clearly stated. Their ethics do not permit "trick" or "catch" questions. Questions may have been tried out on sample groups, or subjected to statistical analysis, to determine their usefulness.

Written tests are often used in combination with performance tests, ratings of training and experience, and oral interviews. All of these measures combine to form the best-known means of finding the right person for the right job.

II. HOW TO PASS THE WRITTEN TEST

A. NATURE OF THE EXAMINATION

To prepare intelligently for civil service examinations, you should know how they differ from school examinations you have taken. In school you were assigned certain definite pages to read or subjects to cover. The examination questions were quite detailed and usually emphasized memory. Civil service exams, on the other hand, try to discover your present ability to perform the duties of a position, plus your potentiality to learn these duties. In other words, a civil service exam attempts to predict how successful you will be. Questions cover such a broad area that they cannot be as minute and detailed as school exam questions.

In the public service similar kinds of work, or positions, are grouped together in one "class." This process is known as *position-classification*. All the positions in a class are paid according to the salary range for that class. One class title covers all of these positions, and they are all tested by the same examination.

B. FOUR BASIC STEPS

1) Study the announcement

How, then, can you know what subjects to study? Our best answer is: "Learn as much as possible about the class of positions for which you've applied." The exam will test the knowledge, skills and abilities needed to do the work.

Your most valuable source of information about the position you want is the official exam announcement. This announcement lists the training and experience qualifications. Check these standards and apply only if you come reasonably close to meeting them.

The brief description of the position in the examination announcement offers some clues to the subjects which will be tested. Think about the job itself. Review the duties in your mind. Can you perform them, or are there some in which you are rusty? Fill in the blank spots in your preparation.

Many jurisdictions preview the written test in the exam announcement by including a section called "Knowledge and Abilities Required," "Scope of the Examination," or some similar heading. Here you will find out specifically what fields will be tested.

2) Review your own background

Once you learn in general what the position is all about, and what you need to know to do the work, ask yourself which subjects you already know fairly well and which need improvement. You may wonder whether to concentrate on improving your strong areas or on building some background in your fields of weakness. When the announcement has specified "some knowledge" or "considerable knowledge," or has used adjectives like "beginning principles of…" or "advanced … methods," you can get a clue as to the number and difficulty of questions to be asked in any given field. More questions, and hence broader coverage, would be included for those subjects which are more important in the work. Now weigh your strengths and weaknesses against the job requirements and prepare accordingly.

3) Determine the level of the position

Another way to tell how intensively you should prepare is to understand the level of the job for which you are applying. Is it the entering level? In other words, is this the position in which beginners in a field of work are hired? Or is it an intermediate or advanced level? Sometimes this is indicated by such words as "Junior" or "Senior" in the class title. Other jurisdictions use Roman numerals to designate the level – Clerk I, Clerk II, for example. The word "Supervisor" sometimes appears in the title. If the level is not indicated by the title, check the description of duties. Will you be working under very close supervision, or will you have responsibility for independent decisions in this work?

4) Choose appropriate study materials

Now that you know the subjects to be examined and the relative amount of each subject to be covered, you can choose suitable study materials. For beginning level jobs, or even advanced ones, if you have a pronounced weakness in some aspect of your training, read a modern, standard textbook in that field. Be sure it is up to date and has general coverage. Such books are normally available at your library, and the librarian will be glad to help you locate one. For entry-level positions, questions of appropriate difficulty are chosen – neither highly advanced questions, nor those too simple. Such questions require careful thought but not advanced training.

If the position for which you are applying is technical or advanced, you will read more advanced, specialized material. If you are already familiar with the basic principles of your field, elementary textbooks would waste your time. Concentrate on advanced textbooks and technical periodicals. Think through the concepts and review difficult problems in your field.

These are all general sources. You can get more ideas on your own initiative, following these leads. For example, training manuals and publications of the government agency which employs workers in your field can be useful, particularly for technical and professional positions. A letter or visit to the government department involved may result in more specific study suggestions, and certainly will provide you with a more definite idea of the exact nature of the position you are seeking.

III. KINDS OF TESTS

Tests are used for purposes other than measuring knowledge and ability to perform specified duties. For some positions, it is equally important to test ability to make adjustments to new situations or to profit from training. In others, basic mental abilities not dependent on information are essential. Questions which test these things may not appear as pertinent to the duties of the position as those which test for knowledge and information. Yet they are often highly important parts of a fair examination. For very general questions, it is almost impossible to help you direct your study efforts. What we can do is to point out some of the more common of these general abilities needed in public service positions and describe some typical questions.

1) General information

Broad, general information has been found useful for predicting job success in some kinds of work. This is tested in a variety of ways, from vocabulary lists to questions about current events. Basic background in some field of work, such as sociology or economics, may be sampled in a group of questions. Often these are principles which have become familiar to most persons through exposure rather than through formal training. It is difficult to advise you how to study for these questions; being alert to the world around you is our best suggestion.

2) Verbal ability

An example of an ability needed in many positions is verbal or language ability. Verbal ability is, in brief, the ability to use and understand words. Vocabulary and grammar tests are typical measures of this ability. Reading comprehension or paragraph interpretation questions are common in many kinds of civil service tests. You are given a paragraph of written material and asked to find its central meaning.

3) Numerical ability

Number skills can be tested by the familiar arithmetic problem, by checking paired lists of numbers to see which are alike and which are different, or by interpreting charts and graphs. In the latter test, a graph may be printed in the test booklet which you are asked to use as the basis for answering questions.

4) Observation

A popular test for law-enforcement positions is the observation test. A picture is shown to you for several minutes, then taken away. Questions about the picture test your ability to observe both details and larger elements.

5) Following directions

In many positions in the public service, the employee must be able to carry out written instructions dependably and accurately. You may be given a chart with several columns, each column listing a variety of information. The questions require you to carry out directions involving the information given in the chart.

6) Skills and aptitudes

Performance tests effectively measure some manual skills and aptitudes. When the skill is one in which you are trained, such as typing or shorthand, you can practice. These tests are often very much like those given in business school or high school courses. For many of the other skills and aptitudes, however, no short-time preparation can be made. Skills and abilities natural to you or that you have developed throughout your lifetime are being tested.

Many of the general questions just described provide all the data needed to answer the questions and ask you to use your reasoning ability to find the answers. Your best preparation for these tests, as well as for tests of facts and ideas, is to be at your physical and mental best. You, no doubt, have your own methods of getting into an exam-taking mood and keeping "in shape." The next section lists some ideas on this subject.

IV. KINDS OF QUESTIONS

Only rarely is the "essay" question, which you answer in narrative form, used in civil service tests. Civil service tests are usually of the short-answer type. Full instructions for answering these questions will be given to you at the examination. But in case this is your first experience with short-answer questions and separate answer sheets, here is what you need to know:

1) Multiple-choice Questions

Most popular of the short-answer questions is the "multiple choice" or "best answer" question. It can be used, for example, to test for factual knowledge, ability to solve problems or judgment in meeting situations found at work.

A multiple-choice question is normally one of three types—
- It can begin with an incomplete statement followed by several possible endings. You are to find the one ending which *best* completes the statement, although some of the others may not be entirely wrong.
- It can also be a complete statement in the form of a question which is answered by choosing one of the statements listed.
- It can be in the form of a problem – again you select the best answer.

Here is an example of a multiple-choice question with a discussion which should give you some clues as to the method for choosing the right answer:

When an employee has a complaint about his assignment, the action which will *best* help him overcome his difficulty is to
    A. discuss his difficulty with his coworkers
    B. take the problem to the head of the organization
    C. take the problem to the person who gave him the assignment
    D. say nothing to anyone about his complaint

In answering this question, you should study each of the choices to find which is best. Consider choice "A" – Certainly an employee may discuss his complaint with fellow employees, but no change or improvement can result, and the complaint remains unresolved. Choice "B" is a poor choice since the head of the organization probably does not know what assignment you have been given, and taking your problem to him is known as "going over the head" of the supervisor. The supervisor, or person who made the assignment, is the person who can clarify it or correct any injustice. Choice "C" is, therefore, correct. To say nothing, as in choice "D," is unwise. Supervisors have and interest in knowing the problems employees are facing, and the employee is seeking a solution to his problem.

2) True/False Questions

The "true/false" or "right/wrong" form of question is sometimes used. Here a complete statement is given. Your job is to decide whether the statement is right or wrong.

SAMPLE: A roaming cell-phone call to a nearby city costs less than a non-roaming call to a distant city.

This statement is wrong, or false, since roaming calls are more expensive.
This is not a complete list of all possible question forms, although most of the others are variations of these common types. You will always get complete directions for

answering questions. Be sure you understand *how* to mark your answers – ask questions until you do.

V. RECORDING YOUR ANSWERS

Computer terminals are used more and more today for many different kinds of exams.

For an examination with very few applicants, you may be told to record your answers in the test booklet itself. Separate answer sheets are much more common. If this separate answer sheet is to be scored by machine – and this is often the case – it is highly important that you mark your answers correctly in order to get credit.

An electronic scoring machine is often used in civil service offices because of the speed with which papers can be scored. Machine-scored answer sheets must be marked with a pencil, which will be given to you. This pencil has a high graphite content which responds to the electronic scoring machine. As a matter of fact, stray dots may register as answers, so do not let your pencil rest on the answer sheet while you are pondering the correct answer. Also, if your pencil lead breaks or is otherwise defective, ask for another.

Since the answer sheet will be dropped in a slot in the scoring machine, be careful not to bend the corners or get the paper crumpled.

The answer sheet normally has five vertical columns of numbers, with 30 numbers to a column. These numbers correspond to the question numbers in your test booklet. After each number, going across the page are four or five pairs of dotted lines. These short dotted lines have small letters or numbers above them. The first two pairs may also have a "T" or "F" above the letters. This indicates that the first two pairs only are to be used if the questions are of the true-false type. If the questions are multiple choice, disregard the "T" and "F" and pay attention only to the small letters or numbers.

Answer your questions in the manner of the sample that follows:

32. The largest city in the United States is
   A. Washington, D.C.
   B. New York City
   C. Chicago
   D. Detroit
   E. San Francisco

1) Choose the answer you think is best. (New York City is the largest, so "B" is correct.)
2) Find the row of dotted lines numbered the same as the question you are answering. (Find row number 32)
3) Find the pair of dotted lines corresponding to the answer. (Find the pair of lines under the mark "B.")
4) Make a solid black mark between the dotted lines.

VI. BEFORE THE TEST

Common sense will help you find procedures to follow to get ready for an examination. Too many of us, however, overlook these sensible measures. Indeed, nervousness and fatigue have been found to be the most serious reasons why applicants fail to do their best on civil service tests. Here is a list of reminders:

- Begin your preparation early – Don't wait until the last minute to go scurrying around for books and materials or to find out what the position is all about.
- Prepare continuously – An hour a night for a week is better than an all-night cram session. This has been definitely established. What is more, a night a week for a month will return better dividends than crowding your study into a shorter period of time.
- Locate the place of the exam – You have been sent a notice telling you when and where to report for the examination. If the location is in a different town or otherwise unfamiliar to you, it would be well to inquire the best route and learn something about the building.
- Relax the night before the test – Allow your mind to rest. Do not study at all that night. Plan some mild recreation or diversion; then go to bed early and get a good night's sleep.
- Get up early enough to make a leisurely trip to the place for the test – This way unforeseen events, traffic snarls, unfamiliar buildings, etc. will not upset you.
- Dress comfortably – A written test is not a fashion show. You will be known by number and not by name, so wear something comfortable.
- Leave excess paraphernalia at home – Shopping bags and odd bundles will get in your way. You need bring only the items mentioned in the official notice you received; usually everything you need is provided. Do not bring reference books to the exam. They will only confuse those last minutes and be taken away from you when in the test room.
- Arrive somewhat ahead of time – If because of transportation schedules you must get there very early, bring a newspaper or magazine to take your mind off yourself while waiting.
- Locate the examination room – When you have found the proper room, you will be directed to the seat or part of the room where you will sit. Sometimes you are given a sheet of instructions to read while you are waiting. Do not fill out any forms until you are told to do so; just read them and be prepared.
- Relax and prepare to listen to the instructions
- If you have any physical problem that may keep you from doing your best, be sure to tell the test administrator. If you are sick or in poor health, you really cannot do your best on the exam. You can come back and take the test some other time.

VII. AT THE TEST

The day of the test is here and you have the test booklet in your hand. The temptation to get going is very strong. Caution! There is more to success than knowing the right answers. You must know how to identify your papers and understand variations in the type of short-answer question used in this particular examination. Follow these suggestions for maximum results from your efforts:

1) Cooperate with the monitor

The test administrator has a duty to create a situation in which you can be as much at ease as possible. He will give instructions, tell you when to begin, check to see that you are marking your answer sheet correctly, and so on. He is not there to guard you, although he will see that your competitors do not take unfair advantage. He wants to help you do your best.

2) Listen to all instructions

Don't jump the gun! Wait until you understand all directions. In most civil service tests you get more time than you need to answer the questions. So don't be in a hurry. Read each word of instructions until you clearly understand the meaning. Study the examples, listen to all announcements and follow directions. Ask questions if you do not understand what to do.

3) Identify your papers

Civil service exams are usually identified by number only. You will be assigned a number; you must not put your name on your test papers. Be sure to copy your number correctly. Since more than one exam may be given, copy your exact examination title.

4) Plan your time

Unless you are told that a test is a "speed" or "rate of work" test, speed itself is usually not important. Time enough to answer all the questions will be provided, but this does not mean that you have all day. An overall time limit has been set. Divide the total time (in minutes) by the number of questions to determine the approximate time you have for each question.

5) Do not linger over difficult questions

If you come across a difficult question, mark it with a paper clip (useful to have along) and come back to it when you have been through the booklet. One caution if you do this – be sure to skip a number on your answer sheet as well. Check often to be sure that you have not lost your place and that you are marking in the row numbered the same as the question you are answering.

6) Read the questions

Be sure you know what the question asks! Many capable people are unsuccessful because they failed to *read* the questions correctly.

7) Answer all questions

Unless you have been instructed that a penalty will be deducted for incorrect answers, it is better to guess than to omit a question.

8) Speed tests

It is often better NOT to guess on speed tests. It has been found that on timed tests people are tempted to spend the last few seconds before time is called in marking answers at random – without even reading them – in the hope of picking up a few extra points. To discourage this practice, the instructions may warn you that your score will be "corrected" for guessing. That is, a penalty will be applied. The incorrect answers will be deducted from the correct ones, or some other penalty formula will be used.

9) Review your answers

If you finish before time is called, go back to the questions you guessed or omitted to give them further thought. Review other answers if you have time.

10) Return your test materials

If you are ready to leave before others have finished or time is called, take ALL your materials to the monitor and leave quietly. Never take any test material with you. The monitor can discover whose papers are not complete, and taking a test booklet may be grounds for disqualification.

VIII. EXAMINATION TECHNIQUES

1) Read the general instructions carefully. These are usually printed on the first page of the exam booklet. As a rule, these instructions refer to the timing of the examination; the fact that you should not start work until the signal and must stop work at a signal, etc. If there are any *special* instructions, such as a choice of questions to be answered, make sure that you note this instruction carefully.

2) When you are ready to start work on the examination, that is as soon as the signal has been given, read the instructions to each question booklet, underline any key words or phrases, such as *least, best, outline, describe* and the like. In this way you will tend to answer as requested rather than discover on reviewing your paper that you *listed without describing*, that you selected the *worst* choice rather than the *best* choice, etc.

3) If the examination is of the objective or multiple-choice type – that is, each question will also give a series of possible answers: A, B, C or D, and you are called upon to select the best answer and write the letter next to that answer on your answer paper – it is advisable to start answering each question in turn. There may be anywhere from 50 to 100 such questions in the three or four hours allotted and you can see how much time would be taken if you read through all the questions before beginning to answer any. Furthermore, if you come across a question or group of questions which you know would be difficult to answer, it would undoubtedly affect your handling of all the other questions.

4) If the examination is of the essay type and contains but a few questions, it is a moot point as to whether you should read all the questions before starting to answer any one. Of course, if you are given a choice – say five out of seven and the like – then it is essential to read all the questions so you can eliminate the two that are most difficult. If, however, you are asked to answer all the questions, there may be danger in trying to answer the easiest one first because you may find that you will spend too much time on it. The best technique is to answer the first question, then proceed to the second, etc.

5) Time your answers. Before the exam begins, write down the time it started, then add the time allowed for the examination and write down the time it must be completed, then divide the time available somewhat as follows:

- If 3-1/2 hours are allowed, that would be 210 minutes. If you have 80 objective-type questions, that would be an average of 2-1/2 minutes per question. Allow yourself no more than 2 minutes per question, or a total of 160 minutes, which will permit about 50 minutes to review.
- If for the time allotment of 210 minutes there are 7 essay questions to answer, that would average about 30 minutes a question. Give yourself only 25 minutes per question so that you have about 35 minutes to review.

6) The most important instruction is to *read each question* and make sure you know what is wanted. The second most important instruction is to *time yourself properly* so that you answer every question. The third most important instruction is to *answer every question*. Guess if you have to but include something for each question. Remember that you will receive no credit for a blank and will probably receive some credit if you write something in answer to an essay question. If you guess a letter – say "B" for a multiple-choice question – you may have guessed right. If you leave a blank as an answer to a multiple-choice question, the examiners may respect your feelings but it will not add a point to your score. Some exams may penalize you for wrong answers, so in such cases *only*, you may not want to guess unless you have some basis for your answer.

7) Suggestions
   a. Objective-type questions
      1. Examine the question booklet for proper sequence of pages and questions
      2. Read all instructions carefully
      3. Skip any question which seems too difficult; return to it after all other questions have been answered
      4. Apportion your time properly; do not spend too much time on any single question or group of questions
      5. Note and underline key words – *all, most, fewest, least, best, worst, same, opposite,* etc.
      6. Pay particular attention to negatives
      7. Note unusual option, e.g., unduly long, short, complex, different or similar in content to the body of the question
      8. Observe the use of "hedging" words – *probably, may, most likely,* etc.
      9. Make sure that your answer is put next to the same number as the question
      10. Do not second-guess unless you have good reason to believe the second answer is definitely more correct
      11. Cross out original answer if you decide another answer is more accurate; do not erase until you are ready to hand your paper in
      12. Answer all questions; guess unless instructed otherwise
      13. Leave time for review

   b. Essay questions
      1. Read each question carefully
      2. Determine exactly what is wanted. Underline key words or phrases.
      3. Decide on outline or paragraph answer

4. Include many different points and elements unless asked to develop any one or two points or elements
5. Show impartiality by giving pros and cons unless directed to select one side only
6. Make and write down any assumptions you find necessary to answer the questions
7. Watch your English, grammar, punctuation and choice of words
8. Time your answers; don't crowd material

8) Answering the essay question

Most essay questions can be answered by framing the specific response around several key words or ideas. Here are a few such key words or ideas:

M's: manpower, materials, methods, money, management
P's: purpose, program, policy, plan, procedure, practice, problems, pitfalls, personnel, public relations

  a. Six basic steps in handling problems:
    1. Preliminary plan and background development
    2. Collect information, data and facts
    3. Analyze and interpret information, data and facts
    4. Analyze and develop solutions as well as make recommendations
    5. Prepare report and sell recommendations
    6. Install recommendations and follow up effectiveness

  b. Pitfalls to avoid
    1. *Taking things for granted* – A statement of the situation does not necessarily imply that each of the elements is necessarily true; for example, a complaint may be invalid and biased so that all that can be taken for granted is that a complaint has been registered
    2. *Considering only one side of a situation* – Wherever possible, indicate several alternatives and then point out the reasons you selected the best one
    3. *Failing to indicate follow up* – Whenever your answer indicates action on your part, make certain that you will take proper follow-up action to see how successful your recommendations, procedures or actions turn out to be
    4. *Taking too long in answering any single question* – Remember to time your answers properly

IX. AFTER THE TEST

Scoring procedures differ in detail among civil service jurisdictions although the general principles are the same. Whether the papers are hand-scored or graded by machine we have described, they are nearly always graded by number. That is, the person who marks the paper knows only the number – never the name – of the applicant. Not until all the papers have been graded will they be matched with names. If other tests, such as training and experience or oral interview ratings have been given, scores will be combined. Different parts of the examination usually have different weights. For example, the written test might count 60 percent of the final grade, and a rating of training and experience 40 percent. In many jurisdictions, veterans will have a certain number of points added to their grades.

After the final grade has been determined, the names are placed in grade order and an eligible list is established. There are various methods for resolving ties between those who get the same final grade – probably the most common is to place first the name of the person whose application was received first. Job offers are made from the eligible list in the order the names appear on it. You will be notified of your grade and your rank as soon as all these computations have been made. This will be done as rapidly as possible.

People who are found to meet the requirements in the announcement are called "eligibles." Their names are put on a list of eligible candidates. An eligible's chances of getting a job depend on how high he stands on this list and how fast agencies are filling jobs from the list.

When a job is to be filled from a list of eligibles, the agency asks for the names of people on the list of eligibles for that job. When the civil service commission receives this request, it sends to the agency the names of the three people highest on this list. Or, if the job to be filled has specialized requirements, the office sends the agency the names of the top three persons who meet these requirements from the general list.

The appointing officer makes a choice from among the three people whose names were sent to him. If the selected person accepts the appointment, the names of the others are put back on the list to be considered for future openings.

That is the rule in hiring from all kinds of eligible lists, whether they are for typist, carpenter, chemist, or something else. For every vacancy, the appointing officer has his choice of any one of the top three eligibles on the list. This explains why the person whose name is on top of the list sometimes does not get an appointment when some of the persons lower on the list do. If the appointing officer chooses the second or third eligible, the No. 1 eligible does not get a job at once, but stays on the list until he is appointed or the list is terminated.

X. HOW TO PASS THE INTERVIEW TEST

The examination for which you applied requires an oral interview test. You have already taken the written test and you are now being called for the interview test – the final part of the formal examination.

You may think that it is not possible to prepare for an interview test and that there are no procedures to follow during an interview. Our purpose is to point out some things you can do in advance that will help you and some good rules to follow and pitfalls to avoid while you are being interviewed.

What is an interview supposed to test?

The written examination is designed to test the technical knowledge and competence of the candidate; the oral is designed to evaluate intangible qualities, not readily measured otherwise, and to establish a list showing the relative fitness of each candidate – as measured against his competitors – for the position sought. Scoring is not on the basis of "right" and "wrong," but on a sliding scale of values ranging from "not passable" to "outstanding." As a matter of fact, it is possible to achieve a relatively low score without a single "incorrect" answer because of evident weakness in the qualities being measured.

Occasionally, an examination may consist entirely of an oral test – either an individual or a group oral. In such cases, information is sought concerning the technical knowledges and abilities of the candidate, since there has been no written examination for this purpose. More commonly, however, an oral test is used to supplement a written examination.

Who conducts interviews?

The composition of oral boards varies among different jurisdictions. In nearly all, a representative of the personnel department serves as chairman. One of the members of the board may be a representative of the department in which the candidate would work. In some cases, "outside experts" are used, and, frequently, a businessman or some other representative of the general public is asked to serve. Labor and management or other special groups may be represented. The aim is to secure the services of experts in the appropriate field.

However the board is composed, it is a good idea (and not at all improper or unethical) to ascertain in advance of the interview who the members are and what groups they represent. When you are introduced to them, you will have some idea of their backgrounds and interests, and at least you will not stutter and stammer over their names.

What should be done before the interview?

While knowledge about the board members is useful and takes some of the surprise element out of the interview, there is other preparation which is more substantive. It *is* possible to prepare for an oral interview – in several ways:

1) Keep a copy of your application and review it carefully before the interview

This may be the only document before the oral board, and the starting point of the interview. Know what education and experience you have listed there, and the sequence and dates of all of it. Sometimes the board will ask you to review the highlights of your experience for them; you should not have to hem and haw doing it.

2) Study the class specification and the examination announcement

Usually, the oral board has one or both of these to guide them. The qualities, characteristics or knowledges required by the position sought are stated in these documents. They offer valuable clues as to the nature of the oral interview. For example, if the job involves supervisory responsibilities, the announcement will usually indicate that knowledge of modern supervisory methods and the qualifications of the candidate as a supervisor will be tested. If so, you can expect such questions, frequently in the form of a hypothetical situation which you are expected to solve. NEVER go into an oral without knowledge of the duties and responsibilities of the job you seek.

3) Think through each qualification required

Try to visualize the kind of questions you would ask if you were a board member. How well could you answer them? Try especially to appraise your own knowledge and background in each area, *measured against the job sought*, and identify any areas in which you are weak. Be critical and realistic – do not flatter yourself.

4) Do some general reading in areas in which you feel you may be weak

For example, if the job involves supervision and your past experience has NOT, some general reading in supervisory methods and practices, particularly in the field of human relations, might be useful. Do NOT study agency procedures or detailed manuals. The oral board will be testing your understanding and capacity, not your memory.

5) Get a good night's sleep and watch your general health and mental attitude

You will want a clear head at the interview. Take care of a cold or any other minor ailment, and of course, no hangovers.

What should be done on the day of the interview?

Now comes the day of the interview itself. Give yourself plenty of time to get there. Plan to arrive somewhat ahead of the scheduled time, particularly if your appointment is in the fore part of the day. If a previous candidate fails to appear, the board might be ready for you a bit early. By early afternoon an oral board is almost invariably behind schedule if there are many candidates, and you may have to wait. Take along a book or magazine to read, or your application to review, but leave any extraneous material in the waiting room when you go in for your interview. In any event, relax and compose yourself.

The matter of dress is important. The board is forming impressions about you – from your experience, your manners, your attitude, and your appearance. Give your personal appearance careful attention. Dress your best, but not your flashiest. Choose conservative, appropriate clothing, and be sure it is immaculate. This is a business interview, and your appearance should indicate that you regard it as such. Besides, being well groomed and properly dressed will help boost your confidence.

Sooner or later, someone will call your name and escort you into the interview room. *This is it.* From here on you are on your own. It is too late for any more preparation. But remember, you asked for this opportunity to prove your fitness, and you are here because your request was granted.

What happens when you go in?

The usual sequence of events will be as follows: The clerk (who is often the board stenographer) will introduce you to the chairman of the oral board, who will introduce you to the other members of the board. Acknowledge the introductions before you sit down. Do not be surprised if you find a microphone facing you or a stenotypist sitting by. Oral interviews are usually recorded in the event of an appeal or other review.

Usually the chairman of the board will open the interview by reviewing the highlights of your education and work experience from your application – primarily for the benefit of the other members of the board, as well as to get the material into the record. Do not interrupt or comment unless there is an error or significant misinterpretation; if that is the case, do not hesitate. But do not quibble about insignificant matters. Also, he will usually ask you some question about your education, experience or your present job – partly to get you to start talking and to establish the interviewing "rapport." He may start the actual questioning, or turn it over to one of the other members. Frequently, each member undertakes the questioning on a particular area, one in which he is perhaps most competent, so you can expect each member to participate in the examination. Because time is limited, you may also expect some rather abrupt switches in the direction the questioning takes, so do not be upset by it. Normally, a board member will not pursue a single line of questioning unless he discovers a particular strength or weakness.

After each member has participated, the chairman will usually ask whether any member has any further questions, then will ask you if you have anything you wish to add. Unless you are expecting this question, it may floor you. Worse, it may start you off on an extended, extemporaneous speech. The board is not usually seeking more information. The question is principally to offer you a last opportunity to present further qualifications or to indicate that you have nothing to add. So, if you feel that a significant qualification or characteristic has been overlooked, it is proper to point it out in a sentence or so. Do not compliment the board on the thoroughness of their examination – they have been sketchy, and you know it. If you wish, merely say, "No thank you, I have nothing further to add." This is a point where you can "talk yourself out" of a good impression or fail to present an important bit of information. Remember, *you close the interview yourself.*

The chairman will then say, "That is all, Mr. _____, thank you." Do not be startled; the interview is over, and quicker than you think. Thank him, gather your belongings and take your leave. Save your sigh of relief for the other side of the door.

How to put your best foot forward

Throughout this entire process, you may feel that the board individually and collectively is trying to pierce your defenses, seek out your hidden weaknesses and embarrass and confuse you. Actually, this is not true. They are obliged to make an appraisal of your qualifications for the job you are seeking, and they want to see you in your best light. Remember, they must interview all candidates and a non-cooperative candidate may become a failure in spite of their best efforts to bring out his qualifications. Here are 15 suggestions that will help you:

1) Be natural – Keep your attitude confident, not cocky

If you are not confident that you can do the job, do not expect the board to be. Do not apologize for your weaknesses, try to bring out your strong points. The board is interested in a positive, not negative, presentation. Cockiness will antagonize any board member and make him wonder if you are covering up a weakness by a false show of strength.

2) Get comfortable, but don't lounge or sprawl

Sit erectly but not stiffly. A careless posture may lead the board to conclude that you are careless in other things, or at least that you are not impressed by the importance of the occasion. Either conclusion is natural, even if incorrect. Do not fuss with your clothing, a pencil or an ashtray. Your hands may occasionally be useful to emphasize a point; do not let them become a point of distraction.

3) Do not wisecrack or make small talk

This is a serious situation, and your attitude should show that you consider it as such. Further, the time of the board is limited – they do not want to waste it, and neither should you.

4) Do not exaggerate your experience or abilities

In the first place, from information in the application or other interviews and sources, the board may know more about you than you think. Secondly, you probably will not get away with it. An experienced board is rather adept at spotting such a situation, so do not take the chance.

5) If you know a board member, do not make a point of it, yet do not hide it
Certainly you are not fooling him, and probably not the other members of the board. Do not try to take advantage of your acquaintanceship – it will probably do you little good.

6) Do not dominate the interview
Let the board do that. They will give you the clues – do not assume that you have to do all the talking. Realize that the board has a number of questions to ask you, and do not try to take up all the interview time by showing off your extensive knowledge of the answer to the first one.

7) Be attentive
You only have 20 minutes or so, and you should keep your attention at its sharpest throughout. When a member is addressing a problem or question to you, give him your undivided attention. Address your reply principally to him, but do not exclude the other board members.

8) Do not interrupt
A board member may be stating a problem for you to analyze. He will ask you a question when the time comes. Let him state the problem, and wait for the question.

9) Make sure you understand the question
Do not try to answer until you are sure what the question is. If it is not clear, restate it in your own words or ask the board member to clarify it for you. However, do not haggle about minor elements.

10) Reply promptly but not hastily
A common entry on oral board rating sheets is "candidate responded readily," or "candidate hesitated in replies." Respond as promptly and quickly as you can, but do not jump to a hasty, ill-considered answer.

11) Do not be peremptory in your answers
A brief answer is proper – but do not fire your answer back. That is a losing game from your point of view. The board member can probably ask questions much faster than you can answer them.

12) Do not try to create the answer you think the board member wants
He is interested in what kind of mind you have and how it works – not in playing games. Furthermore, he can usually spot this practice and will actually grade you down on it.

13) Do not switch sides in your reply merely to agree with a board member
Frequently, a member will take a contrary position merely to draw you out and to see if you are willing and able to defend your point of view. Do not start a debate, yet do not surrender a good position. If a position is worth taking, it is worth defending.

14) Do not be afraid to admit an error in judgment if you are shown to be wrong

The board knows that you are forced to reply without any opportunity for careful consideration. Your answer may be demonstrably wrong. If so, admit it and get on with the interview.

15) Do not dwell at length on your present job

The opening question may relate to your present assignment. Answer the question but do not go into an extended discussion. You are being examined for a *new* job, not your present one. As a matter of fact, try to phrase ALL your answers in terms of the job for which you are being examined.

Basis of Rating

Probably you will forget most of these "do's" and "don'ts" when you walk into the oral interview room. Even remembering them all will not ensure you a passing grade. Perhaps you did not have the qualifications in the first place. But remembering them will help you to put your best foot forward, without treading on the toes of the board members.

Rumor and popular opinion to the contrary notwithstanding, an oral board wants you to make the best appearance possible. They know you are under pressure – but they also want to see how you respond to it as a guide to what your reaction would be under the pressures of the job you seek. They will be influenced by the degree of poise you display, the personal traits you show and the manner in which you respond.

ABOUT THIS BOOK

This book contains tests divided into Examination Sections. Go through each test, answering every question in the margin. At the end of each test look at the answer key and check your answers. On the ones you got wrong, look at the right answer choice and learn. Do not fill in the answers first. Do not memorize the questions and answers, but understand the answer and principles involved. On your test, the questions will likely be different from the samples. Questions are changed and new ones added. If you understand these past questions you should have success with any changes that arise. Tests may consist of several types of questions. We have additional books on each subject should more study be advisable or necessary for you. Finally, the more you study, the better prepared you will be. This book is intended to be the last thing you study before you walk into the examination room. Prior study of relevant texts is also recommended. NLC publishes some of these in our Fundamental Series. Knowledge and good sense are important factors in passing your exam. Good luck also helps. So now study this Passbook, absorb the material contained within and take that knowledge into the examination. Then do your best to pass that exam.

EXAMINATION SECTION

EXAMINATION SECTION
TEST 1

DIRECTIONS: Each question or incomplete statement is followed by several suggested answers or completions. Select the one that BEST answers the question or completes the statement. *PRINT THE LETTER OF THE CORRECT ANSWER IN THE SPACE AT THE RIGHT.*

1. Of the following groups of people, the one that might have the GREATEST difficulty in eating a diet with an adequate intake of protein is

    A. lacto-ovo-vegetarians
    B. strict vegetarians
    C. fruitarians (allow only fruits, seeds, nuts)
    D. lacto-vegetarians

1.____

2. Of the following diet prescriptions ordered by a physician for patients, the one that should alert the dietitian to the need for a conference with the physician to discuss the feasibility of the prescription is

    A. 60 grams protein, 2 grams sodium, 2 grams potassium
    B. 1200 calories, fat controlled, Diabetic
    C. 125 grams protein, 500 milligrams sodium
    D. 1500 calories, 1 gram sodium, Liquid

2.____

3. A hospitalized patient should be encouraged to participate in his own nutritional care. Of the following, the MOST effective tool the dietitian can use to initiate patient involvement is the

    A. selective menu
    B. diet history
    C. home diet instruction
    D. printed diet information sheet

3.____

4. The one of the following which would be *inadvisable* for a dietitian to choose when requisitioning supplementary beverages for a patient on a potassium-restricted diet is

    A. orange juice   B. tomato juice
    C. apricot juice   D. apple juice

4.____

5. Of the dietary recommendations issued by the American Diabetes Association, the MOST important objective in planning the diabetic diet is

    A. restriction of cholesterol and saturated fat
    B. de-emphasis of the traditional carbohydrate restriction
    C. control of caloric intake to achieve ideal body weight
    D. spacing of meals to minimize hyperglycemia

5.____

6. Providing an optimum caloric intake for the patient on a protein-restricted diet presents a major problem to the dietitian when planning a home diet for the patient.
Of the following suggestions, the one that should BEST help solve this problem is to *increase* the patient's intake of

    A. bread and cereals   B. sugar and fat
    C. vegetables and fruits D. meat and poultry

6.____

7. The Recommended Dietary Allowance of the National Research Council is a valuable tool for the dietitian which lists quantities of nutrients which

   A. cover therapeutic nutritional needs of individuals
   B. are normally required by adult males and females, but not by children
   C. are adequate to meet the known nutritional needs of most healthy persons
   D. are revised approximately every 10 years

8. Recent surveys of the nutritional status of hospitalized patients have shown that many patients can be classified as malnourished.
   Of the following activities, the one which is of MOST value to the dietitian in determining whether a patient is malnourished is

   A. recording the patient's height and weight
   B. questioning the patient about past food habits
   C. recording the patient's food consumption in the hospital
   D. assessing the results of routine laboratory examinations

9. Of the following items of information obtained from the patient during the diet interview, the one which would be of LEAST importance to the dietitian when planning a diet program with the patient is the

   A. amount of food consumed
   B. method of food preparation
   C. frequency of meals
   D. age of the patient

10. Of the following, the MOST critical factor involved in planning a diet program with a patient is

    A. accuracy of calculations of amounts of foods allowed
    B. obtaining acceptance of the diet program by the patient
    C. meeting the patient's budgetary allowances
    D. construction of a well-balanced diet

11. Assume that you have been counseling a young diabetic outpatient with a history of frequent hospital admissions for diabetic acidosis. In an attempt to evaluate your success, you reveiw her medical record for the past few months.
    Which of the following items indicates a successful teaching-learning process? The

    A. patient has not lost any weight
    B. patient's personal food records show a well-balanced, adequate intake
    C. patient has not been admitted to the hospital for three months
    D. results of the patient's current laboratory studies fall within normal limits

12. One of the dietitian's concerns is to bring about changes in patients' food habits, where necessary.
    The one of the following techniques which is MOST effective in bringing about such changes is

A. using audio-visual aids to illustrate good nutrition
B. giving individual instruction in principles of nutrition
C. lecturing on good nutrition to groups of patients
D. discussing patients' nutrition problems on an individual basis

13. The hospital dietitian is responsible for recording information relating to the patient's health care on the patient's medical chart.
Of the following, the item that is NOT considered appropriate for recording is the

    A. estimation of daily food intake
    B. comment on dietary restrictions which are unacceptable to the patient
    C. criticism of patient care by other disciplines
    D. request for patient referral to a community agency for diet follow-up at home

14. Suppose that you are preparing a written memo in order to inform your subordinates of a partial change in a work procedure.
Of the following, the clearest way to convey this information is to put in the memo

    A. only the part of the procedure that is changed
    B. the complete old and new procedures
    C. the complete new procedure, incorporating the change
    D. the complete old procedure, and the part that is changed

15. If you are writing a report on the feasibility of changing a dietary procedure which will be read by an administrator, the one of the following which would be BEST for you to do is to make the report

    A. very detailed, including all the minute facts available, thus enabling him to come to his own conclusions
    B. concise, giving him the main facts and your basic conclusions
    C. detailed, giving him all the available information and every possible conclusion
    D. concise, giving him the bare facts, thus enabling him to come to his own conclusions

KEY (CORRECT ANSWERS)

1. C	6. B	11. C
2. C	7. C	12. D
3. A	8. B	13. C
4. B	9. D	14. C
5. C	10. B	15. B

EXAMINATION SECTION
TEST 1

DIRECTIONS: Each question or incomplete statement is followed by several suggested answers or completions. Select the one that BEST answers the question or completes the statement. *PRINT THE LETTER OF THE CORRECT ANSWER IN THE SPACE AT THE RIGHT.*

1. When refrigerating gravy, it is BEST to use

    A. 5 to 10 gallon cooking pots
    B. 20 quart enamel dish pans
    C. 10" by 20" by 4" metal pans
    D. 10" by 20" by 4" enamel pans

2. Of the following measures, the one which is NOT correct is that one pound

    A. equals 453.6 grams
    B. of milk equals 1/2 quart
    C. of white flour equals 4 cups
    D. of butter equals 1 cup

3. The recommended protein intake for the average adult is 1 gram of protein per kilogram of ideal body weight.
   On this basis, the protein requirement for an adult who should weigh 140 pounds is _____ grams.

    A. 54.6   B. 63.5   C. 85.9   D. 140

4. 1000 cc. of a 5% glucose solution contains _____ calories.

    A. 50   B. 75   C. 200   D. 1,500

5. Of the following groups of foods, the one which lists foods all of which are high in iron is

    A. cheese, liver, and lean meats
    B. cheese, green leafy vegetables, and milk
    C. liver, milk, and citrus fruit
    D. liver, green leafy vegetables, and lean meats

6. Of the following groups of foods, the one which lists foods all of which are high in thiamine is

    A. peas, oatmeal, and lean pork
    B. celery, farina, and bacon
    C. oranges, cheese, and turkey
    D. carrots, tomatoes, and beef

7. Of the following vitamins, the one which is MOST important for the oxidation of carbohydrates is vitamin

    A. A   B. B-complex   C. C   D. E

8. Cholesterol occurs MOST abundantly in

   A. peaches, cream, and carrots
   B. cream, cottonseed oil, and liver
   C. cream, liver, and egg yolk
   D. liver, carrots, and egg yolk

9. The HIGHEST percentage of polyunsaturated fatty acids is found in

   A. olive oil   B. butter   C. margarine   D. corn oil

10. Phenylalanine is a(n)

    A. enzyme
    B. hormone
    C. essential fatty acid
    D. essential amino acid

11. A table of composition of foods lists the protein value of a 100 gram portion of hamburger at 22 grams; the protein value of a 45 gram portion of hamburger is, therefore, _____ grams.

    A. 5   B. 9.9   C. 11.3   D. 12.4

12. In trying to control calories, a 13-year-old girl substitutes sweets for adequate amounts of milk, eggs, bread, potatoes, and vegetables.
    Her diet is MOST likely to be deficient in

    A. calories, calcium, and carbohydrates
    B. calories, protein, and calcium
    C. protein, calcium, and iron
    D. protein, carbohydrates, and iron

13. Assume that a patient is being treated for hyperkeratosis caused by a deficiency of vitamin A.
    Of the following groups of foods, the one which it is BEST to add to the diet is

    A. butter and cream
    B. butter and whole wheat bread
    C. cauliflower and orange juice
    D. cauliflower and whole wheat bread

14. Assume that a patient who is pregnant cannot drink milk. The lack of protein can BEST be compensated for by using greater amounts of

    A. noodles and butter
    B. peanut butter and plums
    C. hamburger and legumes
    D. whole wheat bread and carrots

15. If a pregnant woman does not drink milk, the lack of calcium and riboflavin can BEST be compensated for by using greater amounts of

    A. fruits and yellow vegetables
    B. green and yellow vegetables
    C. hard cheese and green leafy vegetables
    D. hard cheese and butter

16. When feeding an aged person, it is usually LEAST desirable to   16.____
    A. allow small frequent feedings rather than 3 meals a day
    B. stress refined, easily digested carbohydrate foods
    C. serve hot food at each meal
    D. serve the largest meal of the day at lunch

17. Of the following, the group of vegetables which should be included on a reducing diet is   17.____
    A. potatoes, lima beans, and okra
    B. corn, beets, and broccoli
    C. asparagus, broccoli, and cauliflower
    D. carrots, baked beans, and parsnips

18. In order to prevent acidosis on a reducing diet, it is MOST important to include a moderate amount of   18.____
    A. iron   B. protein   C. calcium   D. carbohydrate

19. The value of giving a diabetic patient a cup of milk and soda crackers before bedtime is that these foods   19.____
    A. are low in carbohydrates
    B. yield carbohydrates which become available slowly
    C. contain essential amino acids
    D. are easily digestible

20. Patients on a diabetic diet should be told that bacon   20.____
    A. is a meat exchange   B. is a fat exchange
    C. is a bread exchange   D. need not be measured

KEY (CORRECT ANSWERS)

1.	C	11.	B
2.	D	12.	C
3.	B	13.	A
4.	C	14.	C
5.	D	15.	C
6.	A	16.	B
7.	B	17.	C
8.	C	18.	D
9.	D	19.	B
10.	D	20.	B

TEST 2

DIRECTIONS: Each question or incomplete statement is followed by several suggested answers or completions. Select the one that BEST answers the question or completes the statement. *PRINT THE LETTER OF THE CORRECT ANSWER IN THE SPACE AT THE RIGHT.*

1. The one of the following which should NOT be included freely on a 500 mg. sodium diet is
    A. fresh flounder B. frozen fillet of haddock
    C. fresh salmon D. dietetic canned salmon

2. The one of the following which should NOT be included freely on a 500 mg. sodium diet is
    A. tomatoes B. potatoes
    C. beets D. green beans

3. The foods which are MOST effective in stimulating the flow of gastric juice are
    A. white bread and bananas
    B. cream soups and meatloaf
    C. rice and gelatin dessert
    D. meat soups and gravies

4. The group of foods which contributes MOST to the formation of uric acid is
    A. green vegetables and citrus fruits
    B. dried fruits and whole grain cereals
    C. potatoes and eggs
    D. meat and fish

5. The food permitted on a diet which is wheat-free, rye-free, and oat-free is
    A. malted milk B. rice pudding
    C. canned tomato soup D. bologna

6. The one of the following which is usually allowed on a diet for patients with gastric ulcers is
    A. coffee B. whole wheat cereal
    C. roast beef D. bouillon

7. The effect of increasing the percentage of fats in the diet which are composed of polyunsaturated fatty acids is generally to
    A. reduce the cholesterol level of the blood
    B. cure cases of cardiovascular disease
    C. reduce obesity
    D. increase the satiety value of the diet

8. When preparing to draw up a nutrition curriculum for a teaching program for student nurses, your FIRST step should be to

A. determine the relative emphasis to be given each part of the curriculum through analysis of the subject
B. make sure that the necessary rooms and material will be available when needed
C. ascertain the total school curriculum of the student nurses, to avoid unnecessary duplication
D. organize the order in which subject matter should be introduced and determine the techniques to be used

9. The head dietitian's contribution to the nursing curriculum should be MOST concerned with

   A. the chemical and physical properties of food nutrients
   B. the use of foods in the maintenance of health and the treatment of disease
   C. a knowledge of the causes and symptoms of various diseases
   D. effective working relationships between the dietary and nursing divisions

10. Of the following, role playing is MOST suitable as a technique for teaching student nurses to

    A. deal with the poor food habits of aged patients
    B. prepare foods for patients on low sodium diets
    C. recognize symptoms of nutritional deficiency diseases
    D. compute the nutritional adequacy of prepared diets

11. In planning meaningful experiences for student nurses while they are assigned to the dietary department, the BEST experience to include would be

    A. the preparation of simple foods in the therapeutic diet unit
    B. participation in giving therapeutic nutrition instruction to patients
    C. scheduling of food service for patients
    D. observation of the food preparation activities in the main kitchen

12. Assume that, in teaching a lesson to student nurses on applied nutrition, you discover that the entire group lacks knowledge of the basic principles of nutrition.
    It would be BEST for you to

    A. teach the specific action to take in actual case situations instead of the application of principles
    B. advise the students where the basic knowledge can be found and go on with the original lesson
    C. shorten the presentation of the original lesson and allow more time for a question and answer period
    D. teach the basic principles before continuing with the original lesson plan

13. Assume that a shortage of dietitians forces you to assign some tasks to a clerk. Of the following, it would be BEST for the clerk to

    A. plan the work schedule for food service personnel
    B. make up the daily grocery order from the planned menus
    C. train new helpers in sanitary requirements
    D. make up the daily census from patient tray tickets and ward diet orders

14. Of the following, the MOST effective way to reduce waste of food is to

    A. order the highest quality of foods available on the market
    B. prepare cooked foods well in advance of meal time to avoid last-minute use of high temperatures
    C. teach cooks to use standard recipes
    D. prepare fewer salads and vegetables than the amount calculated to be needed, to avoid having any leftovers

15. Assume that there has been an increase in food cost due to waste.
    Of the following ways to try to reduce waste of food, the one which is usually LEAST effective is to

    A. plan a soup or casserole item on the menu frequently in order to use up leftovers
    B. spot-check plate returns to re-evaluate acceptance of menu items
    C. compare the quantity of food being sent to serving units with the actual patient census
    D. check the portions being given in dining rooms and serving areas

16. Because of misuse, an expensive item of equipment, the vegetable slicer and dicer, frequently breaks down and requires repair.
    Of the following, it would be BEST for you to

    A. issue printed instructions on the operation of the equipment to all employees
    B. restrict the use of the equipment to two or three employees, and train them in its proper use
    C. instruct the dietitian to stand near the equipment when in use and observe its operation carefully
    D. keep the equipment locked in a storeroom to prevent the recurrence of damage

17. Assume that a large number of patients and employees in your institution suddenly become ill, and food poisoning is suspected. The one of the following actions which would be LEAST likely to reveal the source of contamination or infection is to

    A. impound samples of foods served during the past 24 hours and send them to the laboratory for analysis
    B. contact as many patients and employees as possible and obtain their food intake history for the past 24 hours
    C. check all dietary employees for the presence of upper respiratory infections and sores or cuts on hands or face
    D. inspect the contents of the food storeroom to determine the age of all canned goods

18. In preparing a budget estimate of the cost of raw food for the coming year, it is LEAST important to consider the

    A. average cost of each meal during the past year
    B. total number of meals to be served during the coming year
    C. estimated number of employees required to prepare and serve food
    D. prediction of food cost trends prepared by the Bureau of Labor Statistics

19. A line organization chart is of value in a dietary department PRIMARILY because it

    A. furnishes information concerning the number of employees required to do each job
    B. supports a request to management for additional employees needed
    C. informs each employee of his days off and his hours of duty
    D. shows the relation of each position in the overall plan of the department

20. Of the following, the BEST use to make of periodic evaluations of employees by their supervisors is to

    A. give a clear picture to the department of each employee's virtues and faults
    B. provide data for selection of employees for more responsible positions
    C. improve the job performance of the employees
    D. let the employees know that their performance is being judged

KEY (CORRECT ANSWERS)

1.	B	11.	B
2.	C	12.	D
3.	D	13.	D
4.	D	14.	C
5.	B	15.	A
6.	C	16.	B
7.	A	17.	D
8.	C	18.	C
9.	B	19.	D
10.	A	20.	C

EXAMINATION SECTION
TEST 1

DIRECTIONS: Each question or incomplete statement is followed by several suggested answers or completions. Select the one that BEST answers the question or completes the statement. *PRINT THE LETTER OF THE CORRECT ANSWER IN THE SPACE AT THE RIGHT.*

1. The orientation of a new dietitian should include instruction in the primary goals of the hospital.
   The MOST important reason for this is that the dietitian

   A. should be able to explain the hospital goals to the kitchen and pantry workers if they ask her
   B. may be able to suggest improvements in hospital operations
   C. should be made to place the hospital's goals ahead of her own goals
   D. will be better motivated if she feels she is helping to fulfill the goals of the hospital

   1.____

2. When training a new employee in a job procedure, it is LEAST desirable to

   A. give him an overall picture of the job and its importance
   B. stress key points when demonstrating the job
   C. have him do the first tryout of the job in your presence
   D. leave him alone once he has completed the tryout successfully

   2.____

3. The method of training should be adapted to the situation. It is BEST to use the conference method, in which the trainees hold a guided discussion among themselves, for

   A. informing dietitians of a new procedure on requisitioning food
   B. instructing student nurses in the foods to be avoided on various therapeutic diets
   C. assisting dietitians to solve problems involving personnel grievances
   D. teaching stockroom workers the proper way of loading and unloading material

   3.____

4. It is LEAST desirable to give detailed instruction sheets describing work procedures to

   A. cooks who are supervised directly and frequently
   B. kitchen helpers whose education is very limited
   C. storeroom workers who perform the tasks involved infrequently
   D. dietitians who are often called upon to exercise independent judgment

   4.____

5. To be sure that an employee who is being trained actually understands his new job, it is BEST to

   A. repeat the training session with him on three successive days
   B. ask him if he understands all the instructions
   C. tell him to ask you if he does not understand any of the instructions
   D. have him repeat the instructions and perform the job

   5.____

6. Several methods of judging the results of training are available to the head dietitian. The one of the following methods which is MOST useful as an indicator of whether a course in improving skills has been effective is to

   6.____

A. ask the trainees their reaction to the course at the close of training
B. test the principles and techniques taught by giving an examination at the close of the training course
C. compare the subjects covered in the lesson plans for the course with the job analysis
D. compare the performance of trainees before and after training

7. A dietitian under your supervision has changed the assignment of a kitchen helper to a less desirable one because he was late twice in one week. You believe her action was premature, and the worker has complained to you of unfair treatment.
It would be BEST for you to

    A. support the dietitian's action when speaking to the helper, but later tell the dietitian to consult you before taking any disciplinary actions
    B. tell the helper that he is under the authority of the dietitian and must accept her decisions
    C. advise the helper that if his future attendance is good, you will see that his previous assignment is restored to him
    D. tell the helper to speak to the dietitian, and discuss privately with the dietitian the principles to follow in disciplining employees

8. Many grievances expressed against a supervisor actually originate outside the work situation; for example, a cook who is worried about his home life may work poorly and continually accuse the dietitian of treating him unfairly. In such a case, you should instruct the dietitian to

    A. keep out of the situation since her actions cannot eliminate the cause of the grievance
    B. advise the cook how to solve the situation which caused the grievance
    C. help the cook to understand that his home situation affects his attitude
    D. listen to the cook's grievance without comment, giving the cook a chance to relieve his tension harmlessly

9. A supervisor is not only part of management, she is also an intermediary with higher management for her subordinates. According to this principle, a head dietitian should

    A. refer employee grievances to higher management for settlement
    B. share with her subordinate employees information from higher management
    C. adapt department directives to meet the circumstances under which her subordinates work
    D. let higher management know of the feelings and desires of her subordinates

10. The mere fact that dietary employees do not complain about their work does not mean that there is a good relationship between them and the supervising dietitian. The BEST explanation of this is that

    A. a happy worker is usually more productive than a discontented one
    B. employees may nurse grievances silently if they do not trust the reaction of the dietitian to their expression
    C. although good relations between the dietitian and dietary employees are desirable, other motivations also spur productivity
    D. we have not yet succeeded in understanding fully why employees act the way they do

11. Assume that the kitchen workers often complain of great fatigue at the end of the day. Your FIRST step should be to

    A. arrange the work schedule to allow rest periods toward the end of the day
    B. arrange the work schedule to have the more fatiguing tasks performed early in the day
    C. obtain more specific facts about where and when fatigue occurs
    D. determine if complaints come from workers who have complained of other working conditions

12. Although you have previously indicated that a dietitian under your supervision should make decisions on her own, she continues asking for your opinion when it is not necessary.
    It would be BEST for you to

    A. continue answering her questions until she feels, capable of making decisions herself
    B. inform her that your function is to supervise her, not to make decisions for her
    C. be less demanding so that she will not fear to make decisions
    D. lead her gradually into making decisions more frequently

13. Employee acceptance of a comprehensive new procedure is MOST likely if the head dietitian

    A. consults the employees when beginning work on the procedure
    B. consults the employees when the procedure is fully formulated
    C. incorporates in the procedure a feature which will benefit the employees
    D. convinces the employees that the procedure will not be made final until it is tried out

14. Because there is a shortage of workers, two cooperative employees assigned to take monthly physical inventory in the food storeroom must also do other tasks and, therefore, continually complete the inventories late. The constant failure to complete the task on time has changed their original enthusiasm for their jobs to discontent.
    It would be BEST for you to

    A. assign no other work to them until each month's inventory is completed
    B. rotate the assignment so that no employee has it too often
    C. make the employees realize you do not blame them for their failure
    D. set the goal for the completion of the inventories at dates the employees can meet

15. An activities report of the dietary department is submitted each month. Several employees are assigned to complete the different parts of the report, a clerk computes the figures, and a typist prepares the final copy. The report is frequently submitted late, although little actual time is involved in the preparation.
    The reason for the delays is BEST ascertained by use of a(n) _____ chart.

    A. line organization
    B. line and staff organization
    C. flow process
    D. employee function

16. In planning a menu for patients, it is LEAST advisable to 16.____

    A. include a crisp, a firm, and a soft food for variety in texture
    B. serve foods which are plain and well-cooked in preference to fancy foods or mixed food combinations
    C. combine flavorful foods with milder ones, in preference to several highly seasoned foods
    D. have foods of one color, for less confusion and greater interest and attractiveness

17. Assume that a dietitian has submitted the following four dinner menus for inclusion in a master menu. 17.____
    The one which BEST demonstrates the basic rules of good menu planning is:

    A. Tomato juice, fried chicken, French fried potatoes, buttered green beans, vegetable relish, bread and butter, jelly doughnuts, coffee, tea or milk
    B. Fruit juice cocktail, baked pork chops with cinnamon applesauce, whipped potatoes, Waldorf salad on lettuce, bread and butter, deep dish apple pie, coffee, tea or mil
    C. Cream of vegetable soup, baked haddock fillet, steamed potatoes, buttered cauliflower, celery hearts, bread and butter, vanilla ice cream, coffee, tea or milk
    D. Vegetable juice, roast beef with natural gravy, mashed potatoes, buttered spinach, corn relish, bread and butter, chilled canned peaches, coffee, tea or milk

18. A head dietitian in a main kitchen must be constantly alert in order to insure that food is being prepared properly for service. 18.____
    For this purpose, it is LEAST important that she

    A. check periodically the time employees begin cooking foods
    B. determine if hot foods are being kept hot and cold foods kept cold
    C. see that the perpetual inventory is posted daily
    D. see that scales are being used for weighing ingredients when needed

19. When setting up standard recipes, it is LEAST desirable _____ for 19.____

    A. the amount of ingredients to be listed in weights and measures
    B. the ingredients to be listed in order of use
    C. each recipe to be set up for 100 portions
    D. fresh food items to be listed as A.P. or E.P.

20. When submitting requisitions for food items, the variety, size, quality, pack, and quantity desired should be specified. 20.____
    Of the following items for requisitions, the one which LACKS necessary information is:

    A. Apples: fresh, McIntosh, 150 per box (approx. 2 1/2" in diam.), Grade A, 80 pounds
    B. Squash: fresh, Grade A, 3 to 5 pound average, in baskets or boxes, 150 pounds
    C. Potatoes: white, Idaho-baking, Grade A, 4 to 6 oz. each, 40 lbs. per box, 6 boxes
    D. Carrots: fresh, Western, topped, Grade B, 2" max. 3/4" min. dia., in sacks, 200 pounds

KEY (CORRECT ANSWERS)

1. D
2. D
3. C
4. B
5. D

6. D
7. D
8. C
9. D
10. B

11. C
12. D
13. A
14. D
15. C

16. D
17. D
18. C
19. C
20. B

TEST 2

DIRECTIONS: Each question or incomplete statement is followed by several suggested answers or completions. Select the one that BEST answers the question or completes the statement. *PRINT THE LETTER OF THE CORRECT ANSWER IN THE SPACE AT THE RIGHT.*

1. Disregarding the cost of labor, it is MORE economical to buy the unprocessed food when   1.____

   A. medium eggs for baking are 76 cents per dozen and frozen whole eggs are 76 cents per pound
   B. fresh peas in the pod are 15 cents per pound and frozen peas are 44 cents per pound
   C. 100 pounds of potatoes in skins are $12 and 30 pounds of peeled potatoes are $3.80
   D. fresh juice oranges are 24 cents per pound and frozen (concentrated) orange juice is $1.50 per 32-ounce can

2. When buying canned foods, it is BEST to purchase an item which is used frequently in large quantities if the   2.____

   A. purchase price per unit would be reduced as a result
   B. space for storage would not be affected to any extent
   C. item is popular with patients and employees
   D. unit-price reduction would be greater than the increase in storage and distribution costs

3. The foods listed below have been ordered for a dinner menu for 350 patients.   3.____
   The one which has been ordered in the MOST NEARLY CORRECT quantity is:

   A. boneless roast beef, 115 lbs.
   B. precooked rice for buttered rice, 15 lbs.
   C. white pearl onions for creamed onions, 200 lbs.
   D. fresh asparagus for buttered asparagus, 50 lbs,

4. Assume that you are serving 4 ounces of pineapple juice for breakfast.   4.____
   The number of cases of 46 ounce cans you would require for 260 employees and 560 patients is

   A. 4   B. 6   C. 10   D. 12

5. Assume that you are to serve 225 employees, 290 patients, 55 staff members.   5.____
   If a #10 can yields 32 servings of applesauce, the number of cases to requisition is

   A. 1   B. 3   C. 4   D. 10

6. You are ordering eviscerated frying chickens to serve a meal of fried chicken to approximately 900 patients and 850 employees.   6.____
   The MOST approximate amount to order is _____ .

   A. 600   B. 1500   C. 2000   D. 2500

7. Of the following vegetables, the one which is MOST acceptable on delivery is

   A. heads of lettuce with 4 or 5 crisp green wrapper leaves on them
   B. broccoli heads with tips of bright yellow showing through
   C. topped carrots that have new sprouts showing on the top
   D. salad greens, such as escarole and chicory, that have a small seed stem in the middle of the head

8. The fresh vegetable which has the GREATEST percentage of waste in preparation is

   A. cabbage   B. celery   C. cauliflower   D. lettuce

9. The tenderness of fryers may BEST be judged by the

   A. firmness of the flesh
   B. flexibility of the breastbone
   C. absence of pinfeathers
   D. weight of the fryers

10. Of the following temperatures for storing fresh foods, the LEAST desirable is

    A. 32° F. for lettuce
    B. 34° F. for beef
    C. 40° F. for eggs
    D. 65° F. for bananas

11. Assume that dishes are to be washed and rinsed in a dishwashing machine and then air-dried.
    The temperature of the water should be _____ F. for wash and _____ F. for rinse.

    A. 160° ; 200°   B. 180° ; 120°   C. 140° ; 150°   D. 140° ; 180°

12. If you are asked to help plan a storeroom for staples and canned goods, you should specify all of the following EXCEPT

    A. a concrete floor with suitable drainage
    B. a room free from machinery, ventilating ducts, and water pipes
    C. enough natural light to allow supplies to be seen easily
    D. only one door, opening into the kitchen

13. If Swiss steak is to be served, it is BEST to use

    A. beef rib
    B. beef loin
    C. bottom round
    D. top sirloin

14. The head dietitian must be concerned with efficiency and with the quality of foods.
    In establishing standard food preparation procedures, it is BEST to recommend that

    A. salad greens for lunch be prepared the previous evening and chilled
    B. potatoes for baking not be sorted by size, to save time and to provide for individual patient preferences
    C. cooked vegetables be placed in the steam table half an hour before the start of the meal to improve the flavor
    D. coffee be made fresh for each meal

15. In order to use a standardized recipe for apple pie throughout the year, it would be BEST to use

    A. frozen apples
    B. fresh sliced apples

C. fresh apples of the same variety
D. canned apples of the same brand name and code number

16. When preparing food, it is LEAST desirable to 16.____

   A. bake pie shells at 400° F
   B. cook egg custard (in water bath) at 325° F
   C. roast prime ribs of beef at 425° F
   D. bake layer cake at 350° F

17. When cooking a tough roast of beef, the method of cooking which should NOT be used is to 17.____

   A. add a little water to the meat and simmer in a covered pan
   B. cook uncovered on a rack in a roaster in the oven
   C. sear until brown and then cook in a pressure cooker
   D. brown, add tomato juice, and simmer in a covered pan

18. When the fat in a deep fat fryer is not hot enough, doughnuts in the fryer 18.____

   A. become soaked with fat
   B. lose their shape
   C. become too soft
   D. develop a dark brown color

19. In order to make BEST use of a deep fat fryer when cooking potatoes, the cook should be instructed to 19.____

   A. fill the fry basket to capacity and place it in the fryer as soon as the fryer is lighted
   B. fill the fry basket to capacity and place it in the fryer when the fat has been heated to the proper temperature
   C. put potatoes in several layers on the bottom of the fry basket and place the basket in the fryer as soon as the fryer is lighted
   D. put potatoes in several layers on the bottom of the fry basket and place the basket in the fryer when the fat has been heated to the proper cooking temperature

20. When using a coffee urn, it is IMPROPER to 20.____

   A. empty the water jacket around the coffee urn after cleaning the urn so that it can dry out thoroughly
   B. draw off coffee into the urn cup and repour through the filter again after water has dripped through the coffee filter
   C. see that the water is boiling before it flows over the coffee grounds into the urn
   D. keep the coffee from boiling after it has been made

KEY (CORRECT ANSWERS)

1. A
2. D
3. A
4. B
5. B

6. B
7. A
8. C
9. B
10. A

11. D
12. C
13. C
14. D
15. D

16. C
17. B
18. A
19. D
20. A

EXAMINATION SECTION
TEST 1

DIRECTIONS: Each question or incomplete statement is followed by several suggested answers or completions. Select the one that BEST answers the question or completes the statement. *PRINT THE LETTER OF THE CORRECT ANSWER IN THE SPACE AT THE RIGHT.*

1. Assume that you have found that coffee served in the doctor's dining room is watery and has grounds in it.
   Of the following, the BEST action for you to take is to

   A. complain to the employee who made the coffee
   B. check with the employee who was responsible for coffee preparation and review the current procedure for coffee making
   C. complain to the supplier about the inferior quality of the coffee
   D. ignore the situation

   1.____

2. If the gelatin dessert planned for the evening meal did not congeal in time, it would be MOST advisable for you to

   A. serve it as is
   B. throw it away
   C. substitute another dessert
   D. omit dessert for this meal

   2.____

3. Of the following, the LEAST necessary information required for a job analysis is

   A. an accurate description of the task to be performed
   B. the desired sequence and probable time required for each step taken
   C. qualifications of the workers on the job
   D. a list of the equipment to be used and the surroundings of the job

   3.____

4. Of the following, the LEAST desirable procedure to follow in caring for an electric food cutter is to

   A. oil the machine once a day
   B. remove the guard, clean the knives and bowl after each using
   C. keep the machine covered when not in use
   D. be sure not to allow water to get into the motor while cleaning the machine

   4.____

5. Of the following, the MOST desirable method for cleaning the meat block is to

   A. soak the entire block in soapy water, then rinse it clean
   B. use a steel scraper or brush, brush thoroughly, and dry wipe the block
   C. use sandpaper and wipe the block clean
   D. wipe it first with a dry cloth, then polish it with an oiled rag

   5.____

6. The ADVANTAGE of using dry milk powder over whole milk is that it is

   A. time saving
   B. cheaper
   C. labor saving
   D. more nutritious

   6.____

7. A GOOD complement to a main dish of cheese is a

   A. side dish of cold cuts
   B. broiled chop
   C. crisp, green salad
   D. juicy roast

8. Raw fruits should be included when planning menus not only because of their vitamin and mineral content but also because of their

   A. low residue content
   B. protein properties
   C. high energy content
   D. laxative properties

9. Cereals are included in the daily menu MAINLY because

   A. they contain proteins of high biological value
   B. of their calcium content
   C. they are a rich source of carbohydrates
   D. of their rich supply of fats

10. Fish should be used at least once a week primarily because it is a GOOD source of

    A. iron
    B. vitamin C
    C. zinc
    D. iodine

11. Milk is pasteurized in order to

    A. increase its fat content
    B. destroy disease organisms
    C. break up the fat globules
    D. increase the vitamin content

12. Milk which has the fat globules dispersed throughout is known as

    A. approved
    B. pasteurized
    C. certified
    D. homogenized

13. Milk is often described as a complete food; however, it contains a POOR amount of

    A. calcium   B. iron   C. protein   D. vitamin A

14. To *purée* means to

    A. cook in a small amount of fat
    B. cut or chop fine
    C. press through a sieve
    D. tear in thin strips

15. To sauté is to

    A. cook in hot fat
    B. cook in oil deep enough to cover
    C. pour fat over the food
    D. fry lightly in a small amount of fat, turning frequently

16. French dressing will, upon standing, separate into two layers because it

    A. does not contain an emulsifying agent
    B. contains an emulsifying agent

C. was not thoroughly mixed
D. contains twice as much vinegar as oil

17. Cooking meats at a low temperature is CHIEFLY advisable because it results in

    A. less shrinkage and greater palatability of the meat
    B. a more well-done product
    C. less waste of water and juices
    D. more gravy

18. A method of cooking by dry heat is known as

    A. blanching   B. frying   C. baking   D. steaming

19. A soup made from two or three kinds of meat, highly seasoned and cleared, is known as

    A. consomme   B. bouillon   C. chowder   D. bisque

20. A pinch of soda added to green vegetables in cookery enhances the green color; however, this procedure is NOT recommended *mainly* because it

    A. hardens the fibers
    B. destroys the vitamins
    C. prolongs the cooking
    D. makes the vegetables less digestible

21. Meat is cooked PRIMARILY in order to

    A. loosen the connective tissue
    B. retain the vitamins
    C. kill the bacteria
    D. coagulate the blood

22. Cake flour is BEST suited for making cakes because it

    A. contains more gluten
    B. is more elastic
    C. contains less gluten
    D. has more water absorbing power

23. A baked custard becomes watery and lumpy if it is

    A. not mixed thoroughly
    B. cooked too long at too high a temperature
    C. too sweet
    D. too salty

24. Of the following types of cake, the one that *usually* does NOT contain any shortening is

    A. chocolate cake   B. angel food cake
    C. spice cake   D. gingerbread

25. Two cases of #5 grapefruit juice will contain _____ cans.

    A. 6   B. 12   C. 24   D. 36

26. The number of tablespoons in a standard cup is

    A. 8 B. 12 C. 16 D. 18

27. Pork of choice quality has a _____ fat.

    A. soft bright red color and brittle
    B. cherry color and pink
    C. grayish color and crumbly
    D. soft grayish-pink color and white

28. *Good* beef should be

    A. pink in color, have light yellow fat, and hard flesh
    B. bright red in color, have creamy white fat, well-marbled, and firm flesh
    C. cherry in color, have hard fat, and firm flesh
    D. pink in color, have soft fat, and hard flesh

29. White potatoes are BEST stored in a

    A. dark, cool, fairly dry place with ventilation
    B. dry, light, well-ventilated place
    C. cold, damp, well-ventilated place
    D. damp, light, well-ventilated place

30. Hominy grits are made from

    A. rice B. wheat C. corn D. oats

31. Fruit juices are BEST classified as _____ beverages.

    A. nourishing   B. reinforced
    C. stimulating   D. concentrated

32. The CHIEF difference in the composition of cocoa and chocolate is their _____ content.

    A. fat   B. vitamin
    C. protein   D. carbohydrate

33. Of the following fruits, the one which is NOT low in fat content is

    A. bananas   B. prunes
    C. apricots   D. avocado pears

34. When toasting a piece of bread, the

    A. protein is changed to proteose
    B. fat is made more digestible
    C. moisture is removed and the surface starch is changed to dextrin
    D. carbohydrate is changed to glucose

35. The MOST important contribution of fruit in the diet is its

    A. vitamin content   B. high caloric value
    C. satiety value   D. acid reaction

36. The number of calories that a diet consisting of 130 grams carbohydrates, 65 grams protein, and 50 grams fat will yield is 36.____

   A. 980   B. 1230   C. 1555   D. 1880

37. The number of grams of protein that a normal, moderately active woman weighing 133 pounds would require daily is *approximately* 37.____

   A. 54   B. 60   C. 68   D. 70

38. Eight grams of fat when oxidized will yield the SAME number of calories as _____ grams of _____. 38.____

   A. eight; protein
   B. twelve; carbohydrate
   C. fourteen; protein
   D. eighteen; carbohydrate

39. A pat of butter weighing 7 grams will give _____ calories. 39.____

   A. 28   B. 63   C. 75   D. 81

40. Two teaspoons of sugar weighing 10 grams will yield _____ calories. 40.____

   A. 16   B. 20   C. 40   D. 50

KEY (CORRECT ANSWERS)

1. B	11. B	21. A	31. A
2. C	12. D	22. C	32. A
3. C	13. B	23. B	33. D
4. A	14. C	24. B	34. C
5. B	15. D	25. C	35. A
6. B	16. A	26. C	36. B
7. C	17. A	27. D	37. B
8. D	18. C	28. B	38. D
9. C	19. A	29. A	39. B
10. D	20. B	30. C	40. C

TEST 2

DIRECTIONS: Each question or incomplete statement is followed by several suggested answers or completions. Select the one that BEST answers the question or completes the statement. *PRINT THE LETTER OF THE CORRECT ANSWER IN THE SPACE AT THE RIGHT.*

1. Of the following, the MOST recent one which is used to relieve patients of their crippling and painful rheumatic symptoms in arthritis is 1.____

    A. insulin   B. thyroxin   C. bile   D. ACTH

2. The organism MOST commonly involved in food poisoning is the 2.____

    A. streptococcus
    B. staphylococcus
    C. salmonella
    D. cl. botulinum

3. Of the following, the one RICHEST in antiscorbutic vitamin is 3.____

    A. citrus fruits
    B. yeast
    C. glandular organs
    D. egg white

4. The anti-sterility vitamin is known as vitamin 4.____

    A. B_1 B. B_2 C. E   D. K

5. Ergosterol, upon irradiation with ultraviolet light, may be converted to 5.____

    A. glucose
    B. vitamin D
    C. glycine
    D. glycogen

6. An INDISPENSABLE amino acid is 6.____

    A. glycine
    B. tyrosine
    C. alanin
    D. tryptophan

7. Of the following foods, the one which is a NATURAL source of vitamin D is 7.____

    A. vegetables
    B. whole grain cereal
    C. fruits
    D. egg yolks

8. The vitamin which influences the calcification of the bone is vitamin 8.____

    A. B   B. C   C. D   D. E

9. Of the following foods, the ones RICHEST in thiamine are 9.____

    A. peas, oatmeal, lean pork
    B. celery, farina, bacon
    C. oranges, cheese, turkey
    D. carrots, tomatoes, beef

10. The chemical name for vitamin B_2 is 10.____

    A. biotin
    B. pyridoxine
    C. nicotinic acid
    D. riboflavin

11. A protein which will maintain life and promote growth is known as a(n) _____ protein.

    A. complete
    B. incomplete
    C. partially complete
    D. partially incomplete

12. Gliadin is an example of a(n)

    A. complete protein
    B. protein hydrolysate
    C. incomplete protein
    D. good quality protein

13. The CHIEF protein in milk is

    A. rennin
    B. lactalbumin
    C. glutin
    D. casein

14. The protein content of milk and egg beverages may be increased by the addition of

    A. bananas
    B. lactose
    C. protein hydrolysates
    D. lanolac

15. The form in which carbohydrate is stored in the body is

    A. glycogen
    B. glucose
    C. sucrose
    D. dextrin

16. Iron is an indispensable constituent of the diet since it is necessary for the

    A. synthesis of insulin
    B. production of thyroid
    C. production of bile
    D. synthesis of hemoglobin

17. To meet the calcium requirement during pregnancy, it is recommended that the diet of a pregnant woman contain

    A. at least two eggs daily
    B. one quart of milk daily
    C. a serving of liver twice weekly
    D. at least two oranges daily

18. Lack of iodine in the diet may result in

    A. gout
    B. simple goiter
    C. arthritis
    D. diabetes

19. Egg yolk from a hard cooked egg is added to an infant's diet at the age of three months CHIEFLY to

    A. compensate for the low iron content of milk
    B. give bulk to the diet
    C. add protein to the diet
    D. compensate for the low fat content of milk

20. Water is important in the diet not only as a solvent and medium for chemical changes but also because it

    A. regulates metabolism
    B. regulates body temperature
    C. stimulates cell respiration
    D. stimulates hormone secretion

21. In addition to human or cow's milk, an infant should be given as its FIRST additional supplement

    A. puréed fruits
    B. egg yolk
    C. cod liver oil
    D. sieved cereal

22. Leafy vegetables should be included in a reducing diet MAINLY because they are

    A. low in carbohydrates
    B. good sources of protein
    C. high in fatty acids
    D. good sources of calcium

23. combination raw vegetable salad may be given on a _____ diet.

    A. low residue
    B. soft
    C. regular
    D. bland

24. Clear soups and bouillon may be taken ad lib by patients on reducing and diabetic diets because they

    A. contain large amounts of minerals
    B. have no fuel value
    C. contain fat which gives a satiety value to the foods
    D. have good protein value

25. The characteristics of a reducing diet for an obese person are low in caloric value,

    A. fat and carbohydrate; normal or high in protein, vitamins, and minerals
    B. fat, carbohydrate, protein, and vitamins
    C. vitamins and minerals; normal or high in carbohydrate
    D. and high in fat

26. The use of mineral oil in low caloric diets should be discouraged because it

    A. interferes with the absorption of all fat soluble vitamins
    B. is completely digestible
    C. contains 9 calories per gram
    D. interferes with the absorption of sugar

27. The diet prescribed for atonic constipation is

    A. *high* in bulk and fiber
    B. *low* in fat and lubricants
    C. *low* in bulk and fiber
    D. *high* in sugar

28. The diet prescribed in Addison's disease is

    A. *low* in sodium and high in potassium
    B. *high* in potassium and low in carbohydrate
    C. *high* in sodium chloride
    D. *low* in sodium and potassium

29. Of the following foods, the one prescribed in generous amounts for a child with celiac disease is

    A. oatmeal
    B. potatoes
    C. peaches
    D. bananas

30. Kempner's rice diet for the treatment of hypertension must be supplemented with   30._____

    A. protein and sodium
    B. butter and fluids
    C. vitamins and iron
    D. fat and protein

KEY (CORRECT ANSWERS)

1. D	11. A	21. C
2. C	12. C	22. A
3. A	13. D	23. C
4. C	14. C	24. B
5. B	15. A	25. A
6. D	16. D	26. A
7. D	17. B	27. A
8. C	18. B	28. C
9. A	19. A	29. D
10. D	20. B	30. C

TEST 3

DIRECTIONS: Each question or incomplete statement is followed by several suggested answers or completions. Select the one that BEST answers the question or completes the statement. *PRINT THE LETTER OF THE CORRECT ANSWER IN THE SPACE AT THE RIGHT.*

1. Of the following foods, the one that a patient on a low sodium diet should AVOID is 1._____

   A. lettuce B. celery C. apples D. milk

2. In planning an alkaline ash diet, the foods that should be OMITTED are 2._____

   A. apples and peaches B. plums and cranberries
   C. almonds and chestnuts D. raisins and carrots

3. A soft diet is 3._____

   A. high in fat
   B. low in residue and readily digested
   C. not readily digested
   D. high in laxative properties

4. The ketogenic diet is 4._____

   A. very high in fat and low in carbohydrate
   B. inadequate in calories
   C. high in carbohydrate and low in fat
   D. adequate in calcium

5. Of the following foods, the one HIGHEST in purine is 5._____

   A. dairy products B. vegetables
   C. glandular organs D. fruits

6. Beriberi is a deficiency disease caused by the LACK of 6._____

   A. carbohydrate B. vitamin B_6
   C. vitamin B_{12} D. thiamine

7. A deficiency in niacin will produce 7._____

   A. anemia B. tetany C. pellagra D. scurvy

8. Dialized milk is prescribed in certain diets CHIEFLY because it 8._____

   A. is high in vitamins
   B. contains practically no sodium
   C. is high in minerals
   D. contains a lot of sodium

9. Milk, cream, and eggs are ESPECIALLY valuable in the treatment of peptic ulcers because they 9._____

   A. increase the secretion of hydrochloric acid
   B. are alkaline forming
   C. have laxative properties
   D. lower the gastric acidity

10. The Grollman diet is used CHIEFLY for treating 10.____
    A. hypertension   B. jaundice
    C. diarrhea   D. ulcers

11. A patient who is allowed only water, clear tea, black coffee, and clear broth is said to be 11.____
    on a _____ fluid diet.
    A. surgical   B. fortified
    C. unrestricted   D. full

12. Of the following foods, the one which a patient sensitive to wheat must AVOID is 12.____
    A. puffed rice   B. milk
    C. gelatin   D. malted milk

13. Of the following foods, the one which a patient on a wheat-free diet may eat is 13.____
    A. rye bread
    B. vegetables with a cream sauce
    C. rye krisp
    D. bran muffins

14. Gelatinization is BEST defined as 14.____
    A. swelling of gelatin in cold water
    B. coagulation of gelatin
    C. coagulation of starch
    D. swelling of starch granules in hot water

15. The symbol A.P., as used in recipes and nutritional charts, means 15.____
    A. always prepared   B. available protein
    C. as purchased   D. always present

16. The symbol E.P., appearing in nutritional value food charts, stands for 16.____
    A. easily purchased   B. edible portion
    C. energy performed   D. easily prepared

17. In writing patients' orders, doctors often use symbols. If a doctor prescribed nourishment 17.____
    for a patient *t.i.d.*, it would mean that the patient was to receive nourishment
    A. once a day   B. three times a day
    C. twice a day   D. as desired

18. The enzyme which brings about the curdling of milk is called 18.____
    A. rennin   B. ptyalin   C. bile   D. pepsin

19. Of the following food sources, the one RICHEST in cholesterol is 19.____
    A. potatoes   B. mackerel
    C. egg yolk   D. oranges

20. The enzyme in saliva which acts on starch is called

   A. rennin   B. pepsin   C. trypsin   D. ptyalin

21. An overdose of insulin is LIKELY to produce

   A. nervousness, excessive hunger, weakness, and sweating
   B. vomiting, labored respiration, and anorexia
   C. polyuria, restlessness, and anhydremia
   D. nausea, labored respiration, and dyspnea

22. One unit of regular insulin will oxidize *approximately*

   A. 2 gms. carbohydrate   B. 2 gms. protein
   C. 3 gms. fat   D. 4 gms. carbohydrate

23. Insulin is a hormone derived from

   A. alpha cells of the pancreas
   B. beta cells of the Islands of Langerhans
   C. bile
   D. thyroid

24. To restore refined wheat flour to approximately the same nutrient level that it was before the flour was milled, the two important nutrients that are added are

   A. calcium and phosphorus   B. calcium and vitamin D
   C. iodine and vitamin A   D. iron and vitamin B

25. Incomplete combustion of fats produces a condition known as

   A. cyanosis   B. avitaminosis
   C. ketosis   D. anoxia

26. Inflammation of the kidneys is known as

   A. nephritis   B. achlorhydria
   C. gastritis   D. jaundice

27. The removal of the nitrogen group from the amino acid molecule is called

   A. deaminization   B. metabolism
   C. nutrition   D. absorption

28. One of the MOST important functions of the liver is to

   A. convert carotene to vitamin C
   B. form bile salts
   C. produce thyroxine
   D. maintain the normal composition of the blood

29. In essential hypertension, there is a(n)

   A. *increase* in systolic pressure and a decrease in diastolic pressure
   B. *decrease* in systolic pressure and an increase in diastolic pressure
   C. *increase* in both systolic and diastolic pressure
   D. *decrease* in both systolic and diastolic pressure

30. The glucose tolerance test is a test used to diagnose

    A. ulcers
    B. hypertension
    C. gallbladder disease
    D. diabetes

KEY (CORRECT ANSWERS)

1.	D	11.	A	21.	A
2.	B	12.	D	22.	A
3.	B	13.	C	23.	B
4.	A	14.	B	24.	D
5.	C	15.	C	25.	C
6.	D	16.	B	26.	A
7.	C	17.	B	27.	A
8.	B	18.	A	28.	B
9.	D	19.	C	29.	C
10.	A	20.	D	30.	D

EXAMINATION SECTION
TEST 1

DIRECTIONS: Each question or incomplete statement is followed by several suggested answers or completions. Select the one that BEST answers the question or completes the statement. *PRINT THE LETTER OF THE CORRECT ANSWER IN THE SPACE AT THE RIGHT.*

1. Foods which are left over may be used by the menu planner CHIEFLY to　　1.____
   A. baste meats
   B. stock the freezer with emergency supplies
   C. provide more variety in the next day's menu
   D. add minerals to the diet

2. When a recipe calls for cooking in a hot oven, it is MOST desirable to set the thermostat at a Fahrenheit temperature of　　2.____
   A. 300°　　B. 350°　　C. 425°　　D. 525°

3. Of the following, the MOST satisfactory method for cooking the less tender cuts of meat is by　　3.____
   A. roasting　　B. broiling　　C. dry heat　　D. moist heat

4. A two-pound chicken is BEST prepared by　　4.____
   A. broiling　　B. stewing　　C. baking　　D. roasting

5. Fats are used in food preparation, *not only* as emulsifiers, *but also* as　　5.____
   A. shortening agents　　B. leavening agents
   C. catalysts　　D. sweetening agents

6. Baking powder is used in cake mixtures CHIEFLY in order to　　6.____
   A. improve the flavor
   B. increase the acidity
   C. lighten the cake and increase its volume
   D. hold the other ingredients together

7. When making a sponge cake, it is important to remember to　　7.____
   A. beat the batter until it doubles in bulk
   B. bake the cake in an ungreased tube pan
   C. bake the cake in a hot oven
   D. remove the cake from the pan as soon as it is baked

8. When making pastry, the fat should be　　8.____
   A. creamed with the flour
   B. first melted and then creamed with the flour
   C. cut into the flour
   D. added to the flour after the water is stirred in

9. Of the following, the procedure which is MOST advisable when cooking dried prunes is to

    A. soak the fruit in hot water to seal in the juices
    B. keep the uncooked fruit under refrigeration at all times
    C. simmer the fruit slowly until it is tender
    D. add sugar to the fruit to improve the flavor

10. Assume that you plan to serve a gelatin dessert for dinner. You have found that gelatin made in the usual way softens in hot weather.
    Of the following, the procedure which is MOST advisable to follow on a warm day is to

    A. thicken the gelatin with cornstarch
    B. substitute a non-gelatin dessert
    C. use fruit juice in the mixture
    D. use less water than usual

11. When preparing cream of tomato soup, it is MOST advisable to

    A. add hot milk slowly to cold tomato juice
    B. mix milk and tomato juice and then heat
    C. add cold tomato juice slowly to hot milk
    D. add cold milk slowly to hot tomato juice

12. In order to prevent cornstarch from lumping in cooking, it is MOST advisable to

    A. mix the starch with cold liquid before heating
    B. add hot liquid immediately to the starch
    C. brown the starch and add hot liquid
    D. heat the starch in a double boiler

13. Of the following, the LEAST desirable way to dry bread is to place it in

    A. uncovered pans on top of heated ovens
    B. paper bags which are suspended over the stoves
    C. deep pans in a warm oven
    D. cabinets which have slow heat

14. Of the following, the one which is a mollusk used in the preparation of soup is

    A. crab   B. oyster   C. lobster   D. cod

15. Whole dry milk is preferable to evaporated milk for use as a beverage CHIEFLY because it

    A. takes less time to prepare
    B. contains more vitamins
    C. can be made to look and taste more like whole milk
    D. contains more calories

16. The one of the following which is a RESIDUE-FREE food is

    A. milk   B. grapefruit sections
    C. lettuce   D. lemon gelatin

17. The one of the following which is NOT a legume is

   A. peanuts   B. okra   C. beans   D. lentils

18. Of the following, the sugar which is SWEETEST is

   A. lactose   B. fructose   C. sucrose   D. maltose

19. Broths are of value in the diet CHIEFLY because they are

   A. high in food value
   B. a good source of protein
   C. effective appetite stimulants
   D. a good source of carbohydrates

20. Of the following groups, the one which may be served on a SOFT diet is

   A. cream soup, mashed potato, spinach puree, toast, butter, custard
   B. broiled chicken, mashed potato, buttered peas, toast, milk
   C. vegetable soup, lamp chops, mashed potato, lettuce salad, toast
   D. clear broth, baked potato, tenderloin steak, carrots, apple pie

21. Of the following fruits, those which may be included in a HIGH ACID ash diet are

   A. prunes   B. oranges   C. bananas   D. pears

22. Of the following statements regarding yeast, the one which is MOST accurate is that yeast

   A. is generally harmful   B. changes starch to sugar
   C. lives without air   D. requires alcohol to live

23. The souring of milk is due PRIMARILY to the action of bacteria on

   A. fatty acids   B. proteins   C. amino acids   D. lactose

24. Glycerol, which is an end product of fat metabolism, is further oxidized in the body to

   A. sucrose   B. galactose   C. levulose   D. glucose

25. Cereals should be included in menus that are planned PRIMARILY to be

   A. weight reducing   B. low in starch
   C. low in cost   D. high in vitamin C

KEY (CORRECT ANSWERS)

1. C
2. C
3. D
4. A
5. A

6. C
7. B
8. C
9. C
10. D

11. C
12. A
13. A
14. B
15. C

16. D
17. B
18. B
19. C
20. A

21. A
22. B
23. D
24. D
25. C

TEST 2

DIRECTIONS: Each question or incomplete statement is followed by several suggested answers or completions. Select the one that BEST answers the question or completes the statement. *PRINT THE LETTER OF THE CORRECT ANSWER IN THE SPACE AT THE RIGHT.*

1. Of the following, a high blood sugar content is MOST likely to be a symptom of

   A. anemia
   B. diabetes mellitus
   C. arteriosclerosis
   D. hypertension

2. Trichinosis is a disease which may be caused by

   A. eating ham which has been overcooked
   B. unsanitary handling of frozen meats
   C. eating food which has been contaminated by infected flies
   D. eating infected pork which has been cooked insufficiently

3. Of the following, the bacteria which causes MOST food poisoning cases is

   A. botulinum   B. salmonella   C. pneumococci   D. streptococci

4. In the normal diet, liver should be used at least once a week since it is a GOOD source of

   A. vitamin C   B. phosphorus   C. iron   D. roughage

5. Water is important in the daily intake of the body CHIEFLY because it

   A. causes the oxidation of food in the body
   B. is a transporting medium for all body substances
   C. cools the air in the lungs
   D. gives off minerals when it is digested

6. Cod liver oil is given to children CHIEFLY in order to aid in

   A. absorption of calcium
   B. carbohydrate metabolism
   C. prevention of beriberi
   D. regulation of osmotic pressure

7. Of the following statements with respect to the nutritional needs of children, the one which is MOST accurate is that

   A. a child of four years of age requires a minimum of 2000 calories a day
   B. it is better for a child to be slightly underweight than to be overweight
   C. proportionately, children require more protein per pound of body weight than do adults
   D. a child whose diet is deficient in vitamin D may develop scurvy as a result

8. The one of the following desserts which it is MOST advisable to use in a low protein diet is

   A. rune soufflé
   B. fruit cup
   C. gelatin
   D. junket

9. The Karell diet is used in the care of

   A. Addison's disease B. cardiac conditions
   C. diabetes D. jaundice

10. Rowe elimination diets are used in cases involving

    A. allergy B. lead poisoning
    C. constipation D. nephritis

11. Of the following conditions, the one for which the normal diet is MODIFIED by restricting sodium is

    A. tuberculosis B. diabetes C. gastritis D. edema

12. The one of the following conditions which may cause jaundice is

    A. faulty functioning of the kidneys
    B. an obstruction in the common bile duct
    C. a deficiency of vitamin C
    D. the presence of the yeast spore

13. It is GENERALLY accepted that exophthalmic goiter may result from

    A. the inability of the body to metabolize purines
    B. injury to the pancreas
    C. a diet deficient in iodine
    D. lack of sufficient sunlight and milk

14. Faulty ossification of the legs, ribs, and cranial bones are symptoms GENERALLY associated with

    A. pellagra B. rickets C. neuritis D. encephalitis

15. Of the following diseases, the one which is characterized PRIMARILY by destruction of the liver cells is

    A. diabetes B. leukemia C. scurvy D. cirrhosis

Questions 16-25.

DIRECTIONS: Column I lists 10 diseases or conditions, numbered 16 to 25, which require dietary treatment. Column II lists the dietary treatments which are generally used for the conditions listed in Column I. In the space at the right, opposite the number preceding each of the conditions in Column I, place the letter preceding the dietary treatment in Column II which is MOST appropriate for the condition in Column I.

COLUMN I

16. Addison's disease
17. cirrhosis
18. diabetes
19. exophthalmic goiter
20. gastric ulcer
21. gout
22. lipoid nephrosis
23. obesity
24. rickets
25. typhoid fever

COLUMN II

A. low carbohydrate diet
B. high caloric, non-stimulating diet
C. non-residue diet, high in protein and acid ash
D. diet high in vitamin C and magnesium
E. high protein, high carbohydrate, low roughage diet
F. high caloric, soft diet, given in small, frequent feedings
G. diet high in carbohydrate and vitamins, low in potassium, with added salt
H. diet with normal or high protein, vitamins, and minerals; low in fat and carbohydrate; low in caloric value
I. high protein and sulphur diet
J. low protein, purine-free diet
K. high protein, low fat diet, with limited sodium
L. diet high in protein and carbohydrate, low in fat, high in vitamin B complex
M. diet high in vitamin D

16. _____
17. _____
18. _____
19. _____
20. _____
21. _____
22. _____
23. _____
24. _____
25. _____

KEY (CORRECT ANSWERS)

1.	B	11.	D
2.	D	12.	B
3.	B	13.	C
4.	C	14.	B
5.	B	15.	D
6.	A	16.	G
7.	C	17.	L
8.	B	18.	A
9.	B	19.	B
10.	A	20.	F

21. J
22. K
23. H
24. M
25. E

EXAMINATION SECTION
TEST 1

DIRECTIONS: Each question or incomplete statement is followed by several suggested answers or completions. Select the one that BEST answers the question or completes the statement. *PRINT THE LETTER OF THE CORRECT ANSWER IN THE SPACE AT THE RIGHT.*

1. In substituting non-fat dried milk for whole milk in a reducing diet, it is important to consider that the dried milk has a lowered content of calories and also a lowered content of

    A. vitamin A
    B. calcium
    C. thiamin
    D. ascorbic acid

2. The PRIMARY role of legumes in our menus is that of providing

    A. economy and variety
    B. protein and vitamins
    C. flavor and color
    D. carbohydrate and protein

3. One pound of body fat is equivalent to APPROXIMATELY _____ calories.

    A. 1000   B. 2000   C. 4000   D. 3000

4. The vitamins present in meat are, in general, limited to

    A. B-complex
    B. vitamin A
    C. ascorbic acid
    D. ergosterol

5. The nutrients MOST commonly lacking in American diets are

    A. ascorbic acid and riboflavin
    B. calcium and vitamin C
    C. protein and carbohydrates
    D. vitamin A and thiamine

6. Glucose and fructose are examples of

    A. disaccharides
    B. polysaccharides
    C. saccharines
    D. monosaccharides

7. Of the following, the food containing a complete protein is

    A. navy beans
    B. almonds
    C. beef round
    D. gelatin

8. The MOST important of the nutritive contributions made by cereals in the diet is their content of

    A. B-complex vitamins
    B. minerals
    C. protein
    D. carbohydrate

9. Loss of vitamin C content during cooking is increased by

    A. excessive stirring
    B. low cooking temperature
    C. low storage temperature
    D. use of a cover on the cooking utensil

10. A research project to improve the world-wide protein deficiency was sponsored recently by

    A. UNICEF
    B. ICNND
    C. India
    D. U.S. Department of Agriculture

10.____

11. An individual with coronary heart disease should

    A. keep the fat intake low
    B. have a high cholesterol intake
    C. eat only hydrogenated fats
    D. have a medium to high sodium intake

11.____

12. Vitamin A is

    A. water-soluble
    B. a precursor of carotene
    C. useful in preventing rickets
    D. fat-soluble

12.____

13. The vitamin A value of carrots is HIGHEST when the carrots are

    A. harvested young as baby carrots
    B. grown in rich loam
    C. mature, of at least 2" crown diameter
    D. cooked in boiling salted water

13.____

14. Loss of nutrients in frozen vegetables frequently occurs when they are

    A. frozen whole   B. dehydro frozen
    C. blanched   D. sliced or chopped

14.____

15. Which of the following foods contains the calcium equivalent to that in one glass of milk?

    A. One-third cup evaporated milk
    B. Three ounces American cheese
    C. One-half cup turnip greens
    D. One dozen soft shelled clams

15.____

16. Which of the following vitamins is NOT water soluble?

    A. Vitamin C   B. Thiamin
    C. Niacin   D. Vitamin D

16.____

17. It is recommended that milk not be subjected to direct rays of the sun because it might destroy one of the following nutrients:

    A. Thiamin   B. Niacin
    C. Riboflavin   D. Pyridoxin

17.____

18. A two-ounce portion of freshly opened canned juice which will contain the largest amount of ascorbic acid is

    A. lemon   B. grapefruit
    C. tomato   D. orange

18.____

19. Baking soda should not be used in vegetable cookery because it

    A. gives a bitter flavor
    B. destroys the chlorophyll
    C. destroys thiamin
    D. destroys vitamin A

20. The toasting of a piece of bread is an example of

    A. gelatinization   B. mastication
    C. carbonation   D. dextrinization

21. A rich source of vitamin K is

    A. butter   B. spinach   C. oranges   D. milk

22. The nutrient losses in the dehydration process are similar to those in

    A. sterilization   B. electronic cooking
    C. evaporation   D. pasteurization

23. A safe daily dietary for a reduction regimen will supply APPROXIMATELY _____ calories.

    A. 2500   B. 1500   C. 2000   D. 3000

24. When a diabetic needing insulin eats more food than his prescribed diet allows, a possible resulting danger is the development of

    A. shock   B. stroke   C. acidosis   D. hemorrhage

25. A good source of riboflavin is

    A. milk   B. onions
    C. vegetable fats   D. orange juice

KEY (CORRECT ANSWERS)

1.	A	11.	A
2.	A	12.	D
3.	C	13.	C
4.	A	14.	D
5.	B	15.	A
6.	D	16.	D
7.	C	17.	C
8.	A	18.	C
9.	A	19.	D
10.	A	20.	D

21. B
22. D
23. B
24. C
25. A

TEST 2

DIRECTIONS: Each question or incomplete statement is followed by several suggested answers or completions. Select the one that BEST answers the question or completes the statement. *PRINT THE LETTER OF THE CORRECT ANSWER IN THE SPACE AT THE RIGHT.*

1. Of the following 100 gram portions of fresh substance, the one which yields the MOST iron is

    A. beef, all lean
    B. egg yolk
    C. dried beans
    D. dried peas

    1.____

2. The following foods tend to diminish acidity in the urine:

    A. Tomatoes, oranges, apricots, pineapple
    B. Tomatoes, cranberries, plums, apricots
    C. Tomatoes, prunes, apricots, pineapple
    D. Cranberries, oranges, apricots, pineapple

    2.____

3. The vitamin MOST readily destroyed in cooking is

    A. vitamin A
    B. ascorbic acid
    C. vitamin D
    D. riboflavin

    3.____

4. The amount of calcium required for a one-year-old child is

    A. less than is needed by a very active man
    B. as much as is needed by a pregnant woman
    C. more than that needed by a very active woman
    D. more than that needed by a ten-year-old child

    4.____

5. The bodily requirement of protein needed by a man on a reducing diet is

    A. less than the amount needed on his normal diet
    B. more than the amount needed on his normal diet
    C. the same amount that is required by an adolescent boy
    D. the same amount that is required on his normal diet

    5.____

6. When food is taken into the stomach,

    A. protein food stays longer than carbohydrate
    B. emulsified fats leave first
    C. mixtures of fat and protein are quickly digested
    D. fat leaves before protein

    6.____

7. Injections of insulin may be needed

    A. to promote oxidation
    B. to raise the concentration of glucose in the blood
    C. to lower the concentration of glucose in the blood
    D. replace adrenaline

    7.____

8. *Depot fat* refers to

    8.____

A. deposits of body fat as reserve fuel
B. fat the body cannot synthesize
C. fat the body cannot re-form
D. fatty acids and glycerols which cannot be re-synthesized by the body

9. An example of a fatty acid is _____ acid.

   A. ascorbic   B. lactic   C. lauric   D. acetic

10. Although milk is said to be the perfect food, it is particularly deficient in one of the following:

    A. Iron
    B. Vitamin C
    C. Vitamin D
    D. Sulfur

11. The number of calories yielded by the anabolism of one gram of carbohydrates is

    A. two   B. four   C. six   D. ten

12. Egg yolk is rich in

    A. manganese   B. calcium   C. phosphorus   D. potassium

13. For normal nutrition, the tissues of the body must be in a state of saturation with respect to vitamin

    A. A   B. B   C. C   D. E

14. In nutrition, the utilization of the absorbed products is called

    A. anabolism
    B. osmosis
    C. metabolism
    D. catabolism

15. The food which will produce an acid ash is

    A. dried beans
    B. carrots
    C. rice
    D. sweet potatoes

16. Carbohydrates are classified chemically according to the number of

    A. oxides
    B. saccharides
    C. hydroxides
    D. carbides

17. The MAXIMUM number of hours during which extracted exposed orange juice will retain effective vitamin C content is

    A. 12   B. 24   C. 36   D. 48

18. Irradiation of foods produces vitamin

    A. A   B. B   C. C   D. D

19. Eggs supplement milk because they provide

    A. protein   B. fat   C. iron   D. vitamins

20. The eating of coarse foods helps in

    A. digesting starches
    B. digesting proteins
    C. preventing constipation
    D. repairing muscles

21. Water is a

    A. regulator of body processes
    B. vitamin-rich food
    C. destroyer of vitamins
    D. fuel food

22. The energy value of the foodstuffs that oxidize in the body can be measured by

    A. calories
    B. body weight
    C. weight of food
    D. quality of the food

23. A good breakfast judged according to growth elements contained in the food would be

    A. orange juice, toast, and coffee
    B. bacon, waffles, and syrup
    C. cereal, milk, rolls, and butter
    D. prunes, cereal, toast, and milk

24. A food that is rich in mineral matter is

    A. white flour
    B. cabbage
    C. butter
    D. ready-to-eat cereals

25. Nutritionally, the BEST way to serve fruits is to

    A. bake them
    B. serve them raw
    C. steam them
    D. stew them

KEY (CORRECT ANSWERS)

1. A		11. B	
2. A		12. C	
3. A		13. C	
4. B		14. C	
5. B		15. C	
6. C		16. B	
7. C		17. B	
8. A		18. D	
9. C		19. C	
10. A		20. C	

21. A
22. A
23. D
24. D
25. B

TEST 3

DIRECTIONS: Each question or incomplete statement is followed by several suggested answers or completions. Select the one that BEST answers the question or completes the statement. *PRINT THE LETTER OF THE CORRECT ANSWER IN THE SPACE AT THE RIGHT.*

1. A rich source of riboflavin is
   - A. turnips
   - B. legumes
   - C. whole grains
   - D. milk and its products

   1.____

2. To promote normal vision is a function of vitamin
   - A. A
   - B. B
   - C. C
   - D. D

   2.____

3. To stimulate the appetite is the function of vitamin
   - A. A
   - B. B_1
   - C. C
   - D. D

   3.____

4. Proteins are classified according to the contained amount of
   - A. oxygen
   - B. carbon
   - C. amino acids
   - D. purins

   4.____

5. Rickets is a deficiency disease due to an insufficient supply of vitamin
   - A. A
   - B. B
   - C. C
   - D. D

   5.____

6. Nicotinic acid is used in the treatment of
   - A. psoriasis
   - B. pellagra
   - C. beri-beri
   - D. scurvy

   6.____

7. Cane sugar is
   - A. invertase
   - B. sucrose
   - C. dextrose
   - D. levulose

   7.____

8. Surplus vitamin A is stored in the
   - A. kidneys
   - B. liver
   - C. blood
   - D. muscles

   8.____

9. Fish liver oils are the richest source of vitamin
   - A. A
   - B. B
   - C. C
   - D. D

   9.____

10. Direct irradiation increases the content of vitamin
    - A. A
    - B. B
    - C. C
    - D. D

    10.____

11. The number of calories yielded by the anabolism of one gram of fat is
    - A. 6
    - B. 7
    - C. 8
    - D. 9

    11.____

12. The LEAST expensive simple sugar is
    - A. levulose
    - B. lactose
    - C. glucose
    - D. galactose

    12.____

13. The element that constitutes the major portion of the weight of the human body is
    - A. copper
    - B. sodium
    - C. calcium
    - D. iron

    13.____

14. The development of the disease known as beri-beri is due to a marked deficiency of vitamin   14._____

    A. A   B. B   C. B_1 D. C

15. Compared with whole cereals, soybeans have   15._____

    A. equal vitamin A values
    B. greater cellulose content
    C. lesser vitamin A values
    D. greater vitamin A values

16. A complete protein found in milk is   16._____

    A. gliadin   B. ovalbumin   C. casein   D. albumin

17. Resistance to infection is a function of vitamin   17._____

    A. A   B. B   C. C   D. D

18. A fat-soluble vitamin is   18._____

    A. A
    B. B_1
    C. C
    D. riboflavin

19. The largest percentage of gluten protein is found in   19._____

    A. oats   B. barley   C. rye   D. wheat

20. The body can produce vitamin   20._____

    A. A   B. B   C. C   D. D

21. The food that will produce an alkaline ash is   21._____

    A. oatmeal   B. eggs   C. oysters   D. bananas

22. Compared with the average reported by the Department of Agriculture for whole grain wheat flour, enriched flour contains iron and thiamine _____ average.   22._____

    A. exactly at the
    B. above the
    C. approximately at
    D. below the

23. The nutrients that can be purchased in the fall at lowest cost per pound of such nutrients is   23._____

    A. kidney beans
    B. oranges
    C. chopped beef
    D. flounder

24. The RICHEST food source of vitamin A is   24._____

    A. milk
    B. egg yolk
    C. spinach
    D. carrots

25. Efficient utilization of both calcium and phosphorus depends on a supply of vitamins   25._____

    A. A, B, E   B. B, D, G   C. A, C, D   D. C, E, G

KEY (CORRECT ANSWERS)

1. D
2. A
3. B
4. C
5. D

6. B
7. B
8. B
9. D
10. D

11. D
12. C
13. C
14. B
15. D

16. C
17. A
18. A
19. D
20. D

21. D
22. C
23. A
24. C
25. C

TEST 4

DIRECTIONS: Each question or incomplete statement is followed by several suggested answers or completions. Select the one that BEST answers the question or completes the statement. *PRINT THE LETTER OF THE CORRECT ANSWER IN THE SPACE AT THE RIGHT.*

1. The part of broccoli which is RICHEST in important nutritive content is the   1._____
    A. stem B. leaf C. flowerlet D. root

2. Vitamin loss in cooking frozen non-acid vegetables is MOST commonly due to   2._____
    A. rapid boiling B. overcooking
    C. leaching D. oxidation

3. Of the following, the only substance which affects the nutritive value of bread is   3._____
    A. yeast B. bread softener
    C. mold inhibitor D. bran

4. The group which contains a foodstuff NOT soluble in water is   4._____
    A. calcium, iron, thiamine, niacin
    B. vitamins B, G, niacin, and C
    C. vitamins A, D, niacin, and E
    D. phosphorus, iron, calcium, iodine

5. *Enriched* flours and breads are wheat products to which have been added specific amounts of thiamin, niacin, and   5._____
    A. iron B. riboflavin and iron
    C. calcium and iron D. ascorbic acid and iron

6. A diet of commonly available foodstuffs will furnish a healthy person more than adequate amounts of all the known essential vitamins EXCEPT vitamin   6._____
    A. A B. B C. C D. D

7. Which of the following should NOT be consumed by someone suffering from hypertension due to its naturally high salt content?   7._____
    A. Celery B. Carrots C. Rice D. Bananas

8. A vegetable source of protein food is   8._____
    A. legumes B. chutney
    C. gelatin D. Irish moss

9. Of the following, a rich source of the vitamin B complex is   9._____
    A. seafoods B. refined cereals
    C. citrus fruits D. whole grains

10. The chemical name for vitamin C is _____ acid.   10._____
    A. cevitamic B. citric C. amino D. lactic

11. Substances which promote growth and energy and help the body resist diseases are

    A. proteins
    B. amino acids
    C. fatty acids
    D. vitamins

12. A ketogenic diet is a diet with a high percentage of

    A. vitamins   B. fat   C. protein   D. minerals

13. Of the following, the LEAST costly, as well as the BEST source of calcium and phosphorus in a form in which it may be assimilated directly, is

    A. dried milk
    B. meat
    C. dried fruits and vegetables
    D. multiple-vitamin-mineral preparations

14. The diet of MOST Puerto Ricans is deficient in

    A. vitamin B and calcium
    B. carbohydrates, proteins, and cellulose
    C. protein, calcium, vitamin A, and riboflavin
    D. fats and carbohydrates

15. Cutting down the amount of cane sugar improves the average diet because sugar tends to

    A. cause diabetes
    B. stimulate the appetite
    C. cause overweight
    D. irritate the digestive tract

16. According to United States law, the percentage of milk fat by weight which butter MUST contain is not less than

    A. 75%   B. 80%   C. 65%   D. 90%

17. Iodine is necessary for the normal functioning of the

    A. red blood cells
    B. thyroid gland
    C. heart
    D. hemoglobin

18. The diet of a 72-year-old woman should include extra quantities of

    A. proteins
    B. vitamins
    C. minerals
    D. carbohydrates

19. Of the following foods, the one which could be included in a low residue diet is

    A. applesauce
    B. mashed potatoes
    C. steamed asparagus
    D. creamed celery

20. As an aid in making up the daily quota of calcium and phosphorus, serve

    A. soda crackers and fruit jelly
    B. pineapple juice to start the dinner
    C. milk puddings as desserts
    D. a peanut butter sandwich at lunch

21. Of the following foods, the RICHEST source of iodine is   21._____

    A. lake trout   B. corn
    C. oranges   D. salmon

22. An element found in proteins but NOT found in carbohy-drates is   22._____

    A. nitrogen   B. carbon   C. oxygen   D. hydrogen

23. Foods such as custards, poached eggs, milk, toast, cereals, puddings, and ice cream are   23._____
    served when the prescribed diet is

    A. bland   B. liquids   C. soft   D. regular

24. Each of the vitamins below is correctly paired with the disease it helps to prevent   24._____
    EXCEPT vitamin

    A. A - pellagra   B. B_1 - beri-beri
    C. C - scurvy   D. D - rickets

25. Of the following, the BEST source of the vitamin which functions to condition the walls of   25._____
    blood vessels is

    A. carrots   B. milk
    C. orange juice   D. whole wheat bread

KEY (CORRECT ANSWERS)

1. B	11. D
2. C	12. B
3. A	13. A
4. C	14. C
5. B	15. C
6. D	16. B
7. A	17. B
8. A	18. B
9. D	19. B
10. B	20. C

21. D
22. A
23. C
24. A
25. C

TEST 5

DIRECTIONS: Each question or incomplete statement is followed by several suggested answers or completions. Select the one that BEST answers the question or completes the statement. *PRINT THE LETTER OF THE CORRECT ANSWER IN THE SPACE AT THE RIGHT.*

1. Body weight can be reduced at the rate of about one pound per week by the daily withdrawal from the bodily stores of about _____ calories. 1.____

    A. 500   B. 1000   C. 2000   D. 3000

2. The availability of iron derived from various sources depends on the 2.____

    A. form in which it occurs in the food
    B. supply of thiamin
    C. amount of iron-rich foods provided
    D. amount of iron required by the body

3. All of the following foods furnish approximately 100 calories EXCEPT 3.____

    A. 1 large orange   B. 1 head lettuce
    C. 1 tbsp. butter   D. 5/8 cup whole milk

4. Excess frost on a package of frozen vegetables indicates 4.____

    A. probable loss of vitamin C
    B. inferior packing
    C. inferior produce
    D. poor air circulation in the freezer

5. Caribbean children find it difficult to adjust to the usual foods of New York City because they are not accustomed to 5.____

    A. fresh fruits   B. rice
    C. fresh eggs   D. fresh milk

6. Dehydration of food by sunlight results in 6.____

    A. loss of vitamin C content
    B. increased bulk
    C. increased vitamin D
    D. lower calcium content

7. Of the following, the one which is MOST economical for protein re-enforcement of the diet is 7.____

    A. egg yolk   B. ice cream
    C. cream cheese   D. skim milk powder

8. The riboflavin content of a food is GREATLY lowered by exposure of the food to 8.____

    A. heat   B. freezing temperature
    C. air   D. sunlight

9. The chemical name for *animal starch* is

   A. glycogen B. glucose
   C. amylodextrin D. dextrose

10. According to the prevailing concept, a diet rich in unsaturated fatty acids can be labeled

    A. anti-atherogenic B. atherogenic
    C. anti-scorbutic D. nephritic

11. Compared with 16-20 year-old girls, 13-15 year-old girls need

    A. less iron B. less vitamin D
    C. more calcium D. more protein

12. To provide vitamin C, serve

    A. apricots B. whole wheat bread
    C. cole slaw D. cocoa

13. Compared with the recommended figure of 50%, the ACTUAL percentage of food calories derived from protective foods in the American diet is

    A. 20% B. 25% C. 33% D. 45%

14. To provide the basis for building red blood corpuscles, feed

    A. cream tapioca B. buttered toast
    C. yolk of egg D. white of egg

15. Salt water fish, as compared with fresh water fish, contain more

    A. iodine B. calcium C. copper D. magnesium

16. As an aid to make up the daily quota of calcium and phosphorus, serve

    A. water at mealtime
    B. milk puddings as desserts
    C. pineapple juice as an appetizer
    D. peanut butter on white bread

17. Potatoes are superior in nutritive value when

    A. cut in strips and fried
    B. cut up and boiled
    C. baked whole
    D. boiled whole without skins

18. An EXCELLENT source of fibrous material is

    A. pureed potato soup B. cream of wheat cereal
    C. mozzarella cheese D. escarole

19. For HIGHEST nutritive value at least cost, of the following choose

    A. meatloaf, soybeans, and vegetables
    B. round steak with brown rice
    C. meatballs and spaghetti
    D. braised mushrooms and liver steak

20. The extractives in meat are valuable because they

   A. provide energy
   B. are a source of iron
   C. supply vitamins
   D. aid digestion

21. Whole-grain cereals are preferred because they

   A. have flavor
   B. are easily prepared
   C. contain vitamins
   D. provide calories

22. The outside leaves of salad greens

   A. contain more vitamin A and iron
   B. make the salad crispy
   C. are more tender
   D. contain more roughage

23. The BEST dessert to provide additional protein in a meal is

   A. apple pie
   B. baked custard
   C. fruit jello
   D. apricot whip

24. Vitamin C is present in _____ milk.

   A. evaporated
   B. pasteurized
   C. raw
   D. condensed

25. The RICHEST vegetable source of riboflavin is

   A. lima beans
   B. fresh peas
   C. lettuce
   D. dried soybeans

KEY (CORRECT ANSWERS)

1.	A	11.	D
2.	A	12.	A
3.	B	13.	C
4.	A	14.	C
5.	D	15.	A
6.	A	16.	B
7.	D	17.	C
8.	D	18.	D
9.	A	19.	A
10.	A	20.	D

21. C
22. A
23. B
24. C
25. C

EXAMINATION SECTION
TEST 1

DIRECTIONS: Each question or incomplete statement is followed by several suggested answers or completions. Select the one that BEST answers the question or completes the statement. *PRINT THE LETTER OF THE CORRECT ANSWER IN THE SPACE AT THE RIGHT.*

1. An effective method for tenderizing meats that are tough is 1.____

    A. braising   B. broiling   C. frying   D. roasting

2. Mutton is obtained from 2.____

    A. lamb   B. hog   C. sheep   D. calf

3. The fibrous material in fruits and vegetables is 3.____

    A. connective tissue   B. pith
    C. cellulose   D. mineral matter

4. When sugar is used in cooking, 4.____

    A. acids soften cellulose
    B. alkalies invert sugar
    C. acids invert sugar
    D. dry heat changes sucrose to glucose

5. Fuel is saved by a 5.____

    A. coal range   B. pressure cooker
    C. gas stove   D. thermos bottle

6. A temperature higher than that of boiling water is obtained in a 6.____

    A. fireless cooker   B. double boiler
    C. steamer   D. pressure cooker

7. RICHEST vitamin D food for a one-year-old child is 7.____

    A. egg yolk   B. homogenized milk
    C. spinach   D. cod liver oil

8. Vitamin A is used in the body to 8.____

    A. stimulate the appetite   B. maintain nerve tissue
    C. resist infection   D. grow bone

9. In making white sauce, 9.____

    A. melt the butter, add flour, then add milk
    B. add butter to hot milk, then add dry flour
    C. mix the flour with hot milk, then add butter
    D. combine fat, flour, and milk simultaneously

10. Baking powder consists of
    A. baking soda, an acid salt, and a starch
    B. iron, carbon dioxide, and fat
    C. baking soda, salt, and starch
    D. carbohydrate, protein, and fat

11. Green vegetables should be
    A. cooked in large amount of boiling salted water uncovered
    B. cooked covered in small amount of boiling water and served at once
    C. started in cold water and brought quickly to boil covered
    D. cooked in small amount of water with addition of soda

12. MOST of the body's vitamin A is in the
    A. lungs   B. kidneys   C. liver   D. muscles

13. A food rich in vitamin C is
    A. plums
    B. celery
    C. green pepper
    D. watermelon

14. The duration of infectious colds has been measurably diminished by administering additional amounts of vitamin
    A. A   B. B_1 C. B_2 D. E

15. Carbohydrate stored in the liver is
    A. galleass   B. glycogen   C. heptarch   D. galactose

16. A quart of milk provides an amount of riboflavin equal to that supplied by lean meat weighing _____ pound(s).
    A. 1/2   B. 1   C. 2   D. 3

17. The number of tablespoonfuls of lemon juice to be added to each cup of sweet milk for a sour milk recipe is
    A. 1/2   B. 1   C. 1 1/2   D. 2

18. When buying boneless meat for one meal, a family of six will need _____ pounds.
    A. 1 1/2   B. 2   C. 2 1/2   D. 3

19. Enamel forming cells of the teeth are sensitive to a deficiency of vitamin
    A. A   B. B   C. C   D. D

20. When invited out to a meal, at the close of the meal
    A. fold your napkin
    B. leave it unfolded
    C. fold it in a roll
    D. leave it on the chair

KEY (CORRECT ANSWERS)

1.	A	11.	B
2.	C	12.	C
3.	C	13.	C
4.	C	14.	A
5.	B	15.	B
6.	D	16.	C
7.	D	17.	C
8.	C	18.	A
9.	A	19.	A
10.	A	20.	B

TEST 2

DIRECTIONS: Each question or incomplete statement is followed by several suggested answers or completions. Select the one that BEST answers the question or completes the statement. *PRINT THE LETTER OF THE CORRECT ANSWER IN THE SPACE AT THE RIGHT.*

1. When buying fish for one meal, a family of six will need _____ pounds.   1.____

   A. 1 1/2   B. 2   C. 2 1/2   D. 3

2. Molasses is rich in   2.____

   A. potassium   B. iron   C. vitamin C   D. niacin

3. The leavening agent in popovers is   3.____

   A. baking powder
   B. steam
   C. baking soda
   D. sour milk and soda

4. A leavening agent used in baking is   4.____

   A. baking soda and sweet milk
   B. sour milk and baking soda
   C. cream of tartar and sour milk
   D. cream of tartar and cornstarch

5. Thiamine is found in   5.____

   A. macaroni   B. rice   C. pork   D. suet

6. In baking a cake, the amount of baking powder needed depends on the   6.____

   A. kind of flour
   B. amount of flour and egg
   C. amount of liquid
   D. acidity of the liquid

7. Vitamin A is MOST concentrated in   7.____

   A. cream
   B. whole milk
   C. skim milk
   D. certified milk

8. HIGHEST in vitamin C is   8.____

   A. egg yolk
   B. soft cooked egg
   C. beef juice
   D. tomato juice

9. Vitamins are lacking in   9.____

   A. butter   B. fruit   C. egg   D. sugar

10. The oil RICHEST in vitamin D is   10.____

    A. mineral oil
    B. olive oil
    C. Crisco
    D. cod liver oil

11. RICHEST in vitamin A is(are)   11.____

    A. beans
    B. onions
    C. Irish potatoes
    D. spinach

12. Chuck steak should be

    A. pan fried   B. broiled   C. roasted   D. braised

13. Sugar in conventional cake method is

    A. sifted with dry ingredients
    B. added to creamed fat
    C. added alternately with flour
    D. added alternately with milk

14. Milk is heated in a double boiler to prevent

    A. curdling   B. burning
    C. coagulation of the protein   D. dehomogenization

15. Soft dough is used for

    A. pie   B. biscuits (baking powder)
    C. cake (butter)   D. muffins

16. Basal metabolism determines

    A. calories in food
    B. carbon dioxide in food
    C. calories required for internal activity of body
    D. ratio of energy to exertion

17. Overweight people have less

    A. need for relaxation
    B. resistance to infection
    C. danger of heart disease
    D. inclination to diabetes

18. A person's weight stays the same if he

    A. eats only enough to supply the energy he uses
    B. exercises daily
    C. rests more
    D. eats more fruits and vegetables

19. Enriched white flour contains

    A. niacin, thiamine, and iron
    B. ascorbic acid and vitamin D
    C. vitamin A and niacinamide
    D. folic acid

20. Pellagra is caused by

    A. bacteria   B. deficiency of niacin
    C. deficiency of iron   D. a virus

KEY (CORRECT ANSWERS)

1. D
2. B
3. B
4. B
5. C

6. B
7. A
8. D
9. D
10. D

11. D
12. D
13. B
14. B
15. B

16. C
17. B
18. A
19. A
20. B

EXAMINATION SECTION
TEST 1

DIRECTIONS: The following groups of sentences need to be arranged in an order that makes sense. Select the letter preceding the sequence that represents the BEST sentence order. *PRINT THE LETTER OF THE CORRECT ANSWER IN THE SPACE AT THE RIGHT.*

1.
   I. The keyboard was purposely designed to be a little awkward to slow typists down.
   II. The arrangement of letters on the keyboard of a typewriter was not designed for the convenience of the typist.
   III. Fortunately, no one is suggesting that a new keyboard be designed right away.
   IV. If one were, we would have to learn to type all over again.
   V. The reason was that the early machines were slower than the typists and would jam easily.

   A. I, III, IV, II, V
   B. II, V, I, IV, III
   C. V, I, II, III, IV
   D. II, I, V, III, IV

2.
   I. The majority of the new service jobs are part-time or low-paying.
   II. According to the U.S. Bureau of Labor Statistics, jobs in the service sector constitute 72% of all jobs in this country.
   III. If more and more workers receive less and less money, who will buy the goods and services needed to keep the economy going?
   IV. The service sector is by far the fastest growing part of the United States economy.
   V. Some economists look upon this trend with great concern.

   A. II, IV, I, V, III
   B. II, III, IV, I, V
   C. V, IV, II, III, I
   D. III, I, II, IV, V

3.
   I. They can also affect one's endurance.
   II. This can stabilize blood sugar levels, and ensure that the brain is receiving a steady, constant supply of glucose, so that one is *hitting on all cylinders* while taking the test.
   III. By food, we mean real food, not junk food or unhealthy snacks.
   IV. For this reason, it is important not to skip a meal, and to bring food with you to the exam.
   V. One's blood sugar levels can affect how clearly one is able to think and concentrate during an exam.

   A. V, IV, II, III, I
   B. V, II, I, IV, III
   C. V, I, IV, III, II
   D. V, IV, I, III, II

4.
   I. Those who are the embodiment of desire are absorbed in material quests, and those who are the embodiment of feeling are warriors who value power more than possession.
   II. These qualities are in everyone, but in different degrees.
   III. But those who value understanding yearn not for goods or victory, but for knowledge.
   IV. According to Plato, human behavior flows from three main sources: desire, emotion, and knowledge,

V. In the perfect state, the industrial forces would produce but not rule, the military would protect but not rule, and the forces of knowledge, the philosopher kings, would reign.

A. IV, V, I, II, III
B. V, I, II, III, IV
C. IV, III, II, I, V
D. IV, II, I, III, V

5.
I. Of the more than 26,000 tons of garbage produced daily in New York City, 12,000 tons arrive daily at Fresh Kills.
II. In a month, enough garbage accumulates there to fill the Empire State Building.
III. In 1937, the Supreme Court halted the practice of dumping the trash of New York City into the sea.
IV. Although the garbage is compacted, in a few years the mounds of garbage at Fresh Kills will be the highest points south of Maine's Mount Desert Island on the Eastern Seaboard.
V. Instead, tugboats now pull barges of much of the trash to Staten Island and the largest landfill in the world, Fresh Kills.

A. III, V, IV, I, II
B. III, V, II, IV, I
C. III, V, I, II, IV
D. III, II, V, IV, I

5.____

6.
I. Communists rank equality very high, but freedom very low.
II. Unlike communists, conservatives place a high value on freedom and a very low value on equality.
III. A recent study demonstrated that one way to classify people's political beliefs is to look at the importance placed on two words: freedom and equality.
IV. Thus, by demonstrating how members of these groups feel about the two words, the study has proved to be useful for political analysts in several European countries.
V. According to the study, socialists and liberals rank both freedom and equality very high, while fascists rate both very low.

A. III, V, I, II, IV
B. III, IV, V, I, II
C. III, V, IV, II, I
D. III, I, II, IV, V

6.____

7.
I. "Can there be anything more amazing than this?"
II. If the riddle is successfully answered, his dead brothers will be brought back to life.
III. "Even though man sees those around him dying every day," says Dharmaraj, "he still believes and acts as if he were immortal."
IV. "What is the cause of ceaseless wonder?" asks the Lord of the Lake.
V. In the ancient epic, The Mahabharata, a riddle is asked of one of the Pandava brothers.

A. V, II, I, IV, III
B. V, IV, III, I, II
C. V, II, IV, III, I
D. V, II, IV, I, III

7.____

8.
   I. On the contrary, the two main theories — the cooperative (neoclassical) theory and the radical (labor theory) — clearly rest on very different assumptions, which have very different ethical overtones.
   II. The distribution of income is the primary factor in determining the relative levels of material well-being that different groups or individuals attain.
   III. Of all issues in economics, the distribution of income is one of the most controversial.
   IV. The neoclassical theory tends to support the existing income distribution (or minor changes), while the labor theory tends to support substantial changes in the way income is distributed.
   V. The intensity of the controversy reflects the fact that different economic theories are not purely neutral, *detached* theories with no ethical or moral implications.

   A. II, I, V, IV, III
   B. III, II, V, I, IV
   C. III, V, II, I, IV
   D. III, V, IV, I, II

   8.____

9.
   I. The pool acts as a broker and ensures that the cheapest power gets used first.
   II. Every six seconds, the pool's computer monitors all of the generating stations in the state and decides which to ask for more power and which to cut back.
   III. The buying and selling of electrical power is handled by the New York Power Pool in Guilderland, New York.
   IV. This is to the advantage of both the buying and selling utilities.
   V. The pool began operation in 1970, and consists of the state's eight electric utilities.

   A. V, I, II, III, IV
   B. IV, II, I, III, V
   C. III, V, I, IV, II
   D. V, III, IV, II, I

   9.____

10.
    I. Modern English is much simpler grammatically than Old English.
    II. Finnish grammar is very complicated; there are some fifteen cases, for example.
    III. Chinese, a very old language, may seem to be the exception, but it is the great number of characters/ words that must be mastered that makes it so difficult to learn, not its grammar.
    IV. The newest literary language — that is, written as well as spoken — is Finnish, whose literary roots go back only to about the middle of the nineteenth century.
    V. Contrary to popular belief, the longer a language is been in use the simpler its grammar — not the reverse.

    A. IV, I, II, III, V
    B. V, I, IV, II, III
    C. I, II, IV, III, V
    D. IV, II, III, I, V

    10.____

KEY (CORRECT ANSWERS)

1. D
2. A
3. C
4. D
5. C

6. A
7. C
8. B
9. C
10. B

TEST 2

DIRECTIONS: This type of question tests your ability to recognize accurate paraphrasing, well-constructed paragraphs, and appropriate style and tone. It is important that the answer you select contains only the facts or concepts given in the original sentences. It is also important that you be aware of incomplete sentences, inappropriate transitions, unsupported opinions, incorrect usage, and illogical sentence order. Paragraphs that do not include all the necessary facts and concepts, that distort them, or that add new ones are not considered correct.

The format for this section may vary. Sometimes, long paragraphs are given, and emphasis is placed on style and organization. Our first five questions are of this type. Other times, the paragraphs are shorter, and there is less emphasis on style and more emphasis on accurate representation of information. Our second group of five questions are of this nature.

For each of Questions 1 through 10, select the paragraph that BEST expresses the ideas contained in the sentences above it. *PRINT THE LETTER OF THE CORRECT ANSWER IN THE SPACE AT THE RIGHT.*

1. I. Listening skills are very important for managers.
    II. Listening skills are not usually emphasized.
    III. Whenever managers are depicted in books, manuals or the media, they are always talking, never listening.
    IV. We'd like you to read the enclosed handout on listening skills and to try to consciously apply them this week.
    V. We guarantee they will improve the quality of your interactions.

    A. Unfortunately, listening skills are not usually emphasized for managers. Managers are always depicted as talking, never listening. We'd like you to read the enclosed handout on listening skills. Please try to apply these principles this week. If you do, we guarantee they will improve the quality of your interactions.
    B. The enclosed handout on listening skills will be important improving the quality of your interactions. We guarantee it. All you have to do is take some time this week to read it and to consciously try to apply the principles. Listening skills are very important for managers, but they are not usually emphasized. Whenever managers are depicted in books, manuals or the media, they are always talking, never listening.
    C. Listening well is one of the most important skills a manager can have, yet it's not usually given much attention. Think about any representation of managers in books, manuals, or in the media that you may have seen. They're always talking, never listening. We'd like you to read the enclosed handout on listening skills and consciously try to apply them the rest of the week. We guarantee you will see a difference in the quality of your interactions.
    D. Effective listening, one very important tool in the effective manager's arsenal, is usually not emphasized enough. The usual depiction of managers in books, manuals or the media is one in which they are always talking, never listening. We'd like you to read the enclosed handout and consciously try to apply the information contained therein throughout the rest of the week. We feel sure that you will see a marked difference in the quality of your interactions.

1.____

2. I. Chekhov wrote three dramatic masterpieces which share certain themes and formats: <u>Uncle Vanya</u>, <u>The Cherry Orchard</u>, and <u>The Three Sisters</u>.
   II. They are primarily concerned with the passage of time and how this erodes human aspirations.
   III. The plays are haunted by the ghosts of the wasted life.
   IV. The characters are concerned with life's lesser problems; however, such as the inability to make decisions, loyalty to the wrong cause, and the inability to be clear.
   V. This results in a sweet, almost aching, type of a sadness referred to as Chekhovian.

   A. Chekhov wrote three dramatic masterpieces: Uncle <u>Vanya</u>, <u>The Cherry Orchard,</u> and <u>The Three Sisters</u>. These masterpieces share certain themes and formats: the passage of time, how time erodes human aspirations, and the ghosts of wasted life. Each masterpiece is characterized by a sweet, almost aching, type of sadness that has become known as Chekhovian. The sweetness of this sadness hinges on the fact that it is not the great tragedies of life which are destroying these characters, but their minor flaws: indecisiveness, misplaced loyalty, unclarity.
   B. <u>The Cherry Orchard</u>, <u>Uncle Vanya</u>, and <u>The Three Sisters</u> are three dramatic masterpieces written by Chekhov that use similar formats to explore a common theme. Each is primarily concerned with the way that passing time wears down human aspirations, and each is haunted by the ghosts of the wasted life. The characters are shown struggling futilely with the lesser problems of life: indecisiveness, loyalty to the wrong cause, and the inability to be clear. These struggles create a mood of sweet, almost aching, sadness that has become known as Chekhovian.
   C. Chekhov's dramatic masterpieces are, along with <u>The Cherry Orchard</u>, <u>Uncle Vanya</u>, and The Three Sisters. These plays share certain thematic and formal similarities. They are concerned most of all with the passage of time and the way in which time erodes human aspirations. Each play is haunted by the specter of the wasted life. Chekhov's characters are caught, however, by life's lesser snares: indecisiveness, loyalty to the wrong cause, and unclarity. The characteristic mood is a sweet, almost aching type of sadness that has come to be known as Chekhovian.
   D. A Chekhovian mood is characterized by sweet, almost aching, sadness. The term comes from three dramatic tragedies by Chekhov which revolve around the sadness of a wasted life. The three masterpieces (<u>Uncle Vanya</u>, <u>The Three Sisters</u>, and <u>The Cherry Orchard)</u> share the same theme and format. The plays are concerned with how the passage of time erodes human aspirations. They are peopled with characters who are struggling with life's lesser problems. These are people who are indecisive, loyal to the wrong causes, or are unable to make themselves clear.

3.
I. Movie previews have often helped producers decide what parts of movies they should take out or leave in.
II. The first 1933 preview of King Kong was very helpful to the producers because many people ran screaming from the theater and would not return when four men first attacked by Kong were eaten by giant spiders.
III. The 1950 premiere of Sunset Boulevard resulted in the filming of an entirely new beginning, and a delay of six months in the film's release.
IV. In the original opening scene, William Holden was in a morgue talking with thirty-six other "corpses" about the ways some of them had died.
V. When he began to tell them of his life with Gloria Swanson, the audience found this hilarious, instead of taking the scene seriously.

3. _____

A. Movie previews have often helped producers decide what parts of movies they should leave in or take out. For example, the first preview of King Kong in 1933 was very helpful. In one scene, four men were first attacked by Kong and then eaten by giant spiders. Many members of the audience ran screaming from the theater and would not return. The premiere of the 1950 film Sunset Boulevard was also very helpful. In the original opening scene, William Holden was in a morgue with thirty-six other "corpses," discussing the ways some of them had died. When he began to tell them of his life with Gloria Swanson, the audience found this hilarious. They were supposed to take the scene seriously. The result was a delay of six months in the release of the film while a new beginning was added.

B. Movie previews have often helped producers decide whether they should change various parts of a movie. After the 1933 preview of King Kong, a scene in which four men who had been attacked by Kong were eaten by giant spiders was taken out as many people ran screaming from the theater and would not return. The 1950 premiere of Sunset Boulevard also led to some changes. In the original opening scene, William Holden was in a morgue talking with thirty-six other "corpses" about the ways some of them had died. When he began to tell them of his life with Gloria Swanson, the audience found this hilarious, instead of taking the scene seriously.

C. What do Sunset Boulevard and King Kong have in common? Both show the value of using movie previews to test audience reaction. The first 1933 preview of King Kong showed that a scene showing four men being eaten by giant spiders after having been attacked by Kong was too frightening for many people. They ran screaming from the theater and couldn't be coaxed back. The 1950 premiere of Sunset Boulevard was also a scream, but not the kind the producers intended. The movie opens with William Holden lying in a morgue discussing the ways they had died with thirty-six other "corpses." When he began to tell them of his life with Gloria Swanson, the audience couldn't take him seriously. Their laughter caused a six-month delay while the beginning was rewritten.

D. Producers very often use movie previews to decide if changes are needed. The premiere of Sunset Boulevard in 1950 led to a new beginning and a six-month delay in film release. At the beginning, William Holden and thirty-six other "corpses" discuss the ways some of them died. Rather than taking this seriously, the audience thought it was hilarious when he began to tell them of his life with Gloria Swanson. The first 1933 preview of King Kong was very helpful for its producers because one scene so terrified the audience that many of them ran screaming from the theater and would not return. In this particular scene, four men who had first been attacked by Kong were being eaten by giant spiders.

4.
I. It is common for supervisors to view employees as "things" to be manipulated.
II. This approach does not motivate employees, nor does the carrot-and-stick approach because employees often recognize these behaviors and resent them.
III. Supervisors can change these behaviors by using self-inquiry and persistence.
IV. The best managers genuinely respect those they work with, are supportive and helpful, and are interested in working as a team with those they supervise.
V. They disagree with the Golden Rule that says "he or she who has the gold makes the rules."

4.____

A. Some managers act as if they think the Golden Rule means "he or she who has the gold makes the rules." They show disrespect to employees by seeing them as "things" to be manipulated. Obviously, this approach does not motivate employees any more than the carrot-and-stick approach motivates them. The employees are smart enough to spot these behaviors and resent them. On the other hand, the managers genuinely respect those they work with, are supportive and helpful, and are interested in working as a team. Self-inquiry and persistence can change even the former type of supervisor into the latter.

B. Many supervisors fall into the trap of viewing employees as "things" to be manipulated, or try to motivate them by using a carrot-and-stick approach. These methods do not motivate employees, who often recognize the behaviors and resent them. Supervisors can change these behaviors, however, by using self-inquiry and persistence. The best managers are supportive and helpful, and have genuine respect for those with whom they work. They are interested in working as a team with those they supervise. To them, the Golden Rule is not "he or she who has the gold makes the rules."

C. Some supervisors see employees as "things" to be used or manipulated using a carrot-and-stick technique. These methods don't work. Employees often see through them and resent them. A supervisor who wants to change may do so. The techniques of self-inquiry and persistence can be used to turn him or her into the type of supervisor who doesn't think the Golden Rule is "he or she who has the gold makes the rules." They may become like the best managers who treat those with whom they work with respect and give them help and support. These are the managers who know how to build a team.

D. Unfortunately, many supervisors act as if their employees are objects whose movements they can position at will. This mistaken belief has the same result as another popular motivational technique — the carrot-and-stick approach. Both attitudes can lead to the same result — resentment from those employees who recognize the behaviors for what they are. Supervisors who recognize these behaviors can change through the use of persistence and the use of self-inquiry. It's important to remember that the best managers respect their employees. They readily give necessary help and support and are interested in working as a team with those they supervise. To these managers, the Golden Rule is not "he or she who has the gold makes the rules."

5.
I. The first half of the nineteenth century produced a group of pessimistic poets — Byron, De Musset, Heine, Pushkin, and Leopardi.
II. It also produced a group of pessimistic composers — Schubert, Chopin, Schumann, and even the later Beethoven.
III. Above all, in philosophy, there was the profoundly pessimistic philosopher, Schopenhauer.
IV. The Revolution was dead, the Bourbons were restored, the feudal barons were reclaiming their land, and progress everywhere was being suppressed, as the great age was over.
V. "I thank God," said Goethe, "that I am not young in so thoroughly finished a world."

A. "I thank God," said Goethe, "that I am not young in so thoroughly finished a world." The Revolution was dead, the Bourbons were restored, the feudal barons were reclaiming their land, and progress everywhere was being suppressed. The first half of the nineteenth century produced a group of pessimistic poets: Byron, De Musset, Heine, Pushkin, and Leopardi. It also produced pessimistic composers: Schubert, Chopin, Schumann. Although Beethoven came later, he fits into this group, too. Finally and above all, it also produced a profoundly pessimistic philosopher, Schopenhauer. The great age was over.

B. The first half of the nineteenth century produced a group of pessimistic poets: Byron, De Musset, Heine, Pushkin, and Leopardi. It produced a group of pessimistic composers: Schubert, Chopin, Schumann, and even the later Beethoven. Above all, it produced a profoundly pessimistic philosopher, Schopenhauer. For each of these men, the great age was over. The Revolution was dead, and the Bourbons were restored. The feudal barons were reclaiming their land, and progress everywhere was being suppressed.

C. The great age was over. The Revolution was dead—the Bourbons were restored, and the feudal barons were reclaiming their land. Progress everywhere was being suppressed. Out of this climate came a profound pessimism. Poets, like Byron, De Musset, Heine, Pushkin, and Leopardi; composers, like Schubert, Chopin, Schumann, and even the later Beethoven; and, above all, a profoundly pessimistic philosopher, Schopenauer. This pessimism which arose in the first half of the nineteenth century is illustrated by these words of Goethe, "I thank God that I am not young in so thoroughly finished a world."

D. The first half of the nineteenth century produced a group of pessimistic poets, Byron, De Musset, Heine, Pushkin, and Leopardi — and a group of pessimistic composers, Schubert, Chopin, Schumann, and the later Beethoven. Above all, it produced a profoundly pessimistic philosopher, Schopenhauer. The great age was over. The Revolution was dead, the Bourbons were restored, the feudal barons were reclaiming their land, and progress everywhere was being suppressed. "I thank God," said Goethe, "that I am not young in so thoroughly finished a world."

5.____

6.
I. A new manager sometimes may feel insecure about his or her competence in the new position.
II. The new manager may then exhibit defensive or arrogant behavior towards those one supervises, or the new manager may direct overly flattering behavior toward one's new supervisor.

6.____

A. Sometimes, a new manager may feel insecure about his or her ability to perform well in this new position. The insecurity may lead him or her to treat others differently. He or she may display arrogant or defensive behavior towards those he or she supervises, or be overly flattering to his or her new supervisor.
B. A new manager may sometimes feel insecure about his or her ability to perform well in the new position. He or she may then become arrogant, defensive, or overly flattering towards those he or she works with.
C. There are times when a new manager may be insecure about how well he or she can perform in the new job. The new manager may also behave defensive or act in an arrogant way towards those he or she supervises, or overly flatter his or her boss.
D. Sometimes, a new manager may feel insecure about his or her ability to perform well in the new position. He or she may then display arrogant or defensive behavior towards those they supervise, or become overly flattering towards their supervisors.

7.
I. It is possible to eliminate unwanted behavior by bringing it under stimulus control — tying the behavior to a cue, and then never, or rarely, giving the cue.
II. One trainer successfully used this method to keep an energetic young porpoise from coming out of her tank whenever she felt like it, which was potentially dangerous.
III. Her trainer taught her to do it for a reward, in response to a hand signal, and then rarely gave the signal.

7._____

A. Unwanted behavior can be eliminated by tying the behavior to a cue, and then never, or rarely, giving the cue. This is called stimulus control. One trainer was able to use this method to keep an energetic young porpoise from coming out of her tank by teaching her to come out for a reward in response to a hand signal, and then rarely giving the signal.
B. Stimulus control can be used to eliminate unwanted behavior. In this method, behavior is tied to a cue, and then the cue is rarely, if ever, given. One trainer was able to successfully use stimulus control to keep an energetic young porpoise from coming out of her tank whenever she felt like it — a potentially dangerous practice. She taught the porpoise to come out for a reward when she gave a hand signal, and then rarely gave the signal.
C. It is possible to eliminate behavior that is undesirable by bringing it under stimulus control by tying behavior to a signal, and then rarely giving the signal. One trainer successfully used this method to keep an energetic young porpoise from coming out of her tank, a potentially dangerous situation. Her trainer taught the porpoise to do it for a reward, in response to a hand signal, and then would rarely give the signal.
D. By using stimulus control, it is possible to eliminate unwanted behavior by tying the behavior to a cue, and then rarely or never give the cue. One trainer was able to use this method to successfully stop a young porpoise from coming out of her tank whenever she felt like it. To curb this potentially dangerous practice, the porpoise was taught by the trainer to come out of the tank for a reward, in response to a hand signal, and then rarely given the signal.

8. I. There is a great deal of concern over the safety of commercial trucks, caused by their greatly increased role in serious accidents since federal deregulation in 1981.
    II. Recently, 60 percent of trucks in New York and Connecticut and 70 percent of trucks in Maryland randomly stopped by state troopers failed safety inspections.
    III. Sixteen states in the United States require no training at all for truck drivers.

    A. Since federal deregulation in 1981, there has been a great deal of concern over the safety of commercial trucks, and their greatly increased role in serious accidents. Recently, 60 percent of trucks in New York and Connecticut, and 70 percent of trucks in Maryland failed safety inspections. Sixteen states in the United States require no training at all for truck drivers.
    B. There is a great deal of concern over the safety of commercial trucks since federal deregulation in 1981. Their role in serious accidents has greatly increased. Recently, 60 percent of trucks randomly stopped in Connecticut and New York, and 70 percent in Maryland failed safety inspections conducted by state troopers. Sixteen states in the United States provide no training at all for truck drivers.
    C. Commercial trucks have a greatly increased role in serious accidents since federal deregulation in 1981. This has led to a great deal of concern. Recently, 70 percent of trucks in Maryland and 60 percent of trucks in New York and Connecticut failed inspection of those that were randomly stopped by state troopers. Sixteen states in the United States require no training for all truck drivers.
    D. Since federal deregulation in 1981, the role that commercial trucks have played in serious accidents has greatly increased, and this has led to a great deal of concern. Recently, 60 percent of trucks in New York and Connecticut, and 70 percent of trucks in Maryland randomly stopped by state troopers failed safety inspections. Sixteen states in the U.S. don't require any training for truck drivers.

9. I. No matter how much some people have, they still feel unsatisfied and want more, or want to keep what they have forever.
    II. One recent television documentary showed several people flying from New York to Paris for a one-day shopping spree to buy platinum earrings, because they were bored.
    III. In Brazil, some people are ordering coffins that cost a minimum of $45,000 and are equipping them with deluxe stereos, televisions and other graveyard necessities.

    A. Some people, despite having a great deal, still feel unsatisfied and want more, or think they can keep what they have forever. One recent documentary on television showed several people enroute from Paris to New York for a one day shopping spree to buy platinum earrings, because they were bored. Some people in Brazil are even ordering coffins equipped with such graveyard necessities as deluxe stereos and televisions. The price of the coffins start at $45,000.
    B. No matter how much some people have, they may feel unsatisfied. This leads them to want more, or to want to keep what they have forever. Recently, a television documentary depicting several people flying from New York to Paris for a one day shopping spree to buy platinum earrings. They were bored. Some people in Brazil are ordering coffins that cost at least $45,000 and come equipped with deluxe televisions, stereos and other necessary graveyard items.
    C. Some people will be dissatisfied no matter how much they have. They may want more, or they may want to keep what they have forever. One recent television documentary showed several people, motivated by boredom, jetting from New York to

Paris for a one-day shopping spree to buy platinum earrings. In Brazil, some people are ordering coffins equipped with deluxe stereos, televisions and other graveyard necessities. The minimum price for these coffins - $45,000.

D. Some people are never satisfied. No matter how much they have they still want more, or think they can keep what they have forever. One television documentary recently showed several people flying from New York to Paris for the day to buy platinum earrings because they were bored. In Brazil, some people are ordering coffins that cost $45,000 and are equipped with deluxe stereos, televisions and other graveyard necessities.

10.
I. A television signal or Video signal has three parts.
II. Its parts are the black-and-white portion, the color portion, and the synchronizing (sync) pulses, which keep the picture stable.
III. Each video source, whether it's a camera or a video-cassette recorder, contains its own generator of these synchronizing pulses to accompany the picture that it's sending in order to keep it steady and straight.
IV. In order to produce a clean recording, a video-cassette recorder must "lock-up" to the sync pulses that are part of the video it is trying to record, and this effort may be very noticeable if the device does not have genlock.

A. There are three parts to a television or video signal: the black-and-white part, the color part, and the synchronizing (sync) pulses, which keep the picture stable. Whether it's a video-cassette recorder or a camera, each each video source contains its own pulse that synchronizes and generates the picture it's sending in order to keep it straight and steady. A video-cassette recorder must "lock up" to the sync pulses that are part of the video it's trying to record. If the device doesn't have genlock, this effort must be very noticeable.
B. A video signal or television is comprised of three parts: the black-and-white portion, the color portion, and the the sync (synchronizing) pulses, which keep the picture stable. Whether it's a camera or a video-cassette recorder, each video source contains its own generator of these synchronizing pulses. These accompany the picture that it's sending in order to keep it straight and steady. A video-cassette recorder must "lock up" to the sync pulses that are part of the video it is trying to record in order to produce a clean recording. This effort may be very noticeable if the device does not have genlock.
C. There are three parts to a television or video signal: the color portion, the black-and-white portion, and the sync (synchronizing pulses). These keep the picture stable. Each video source, whether it's a video-cassette recorder or a camera, generates these synchronizing pulses accompanying the picture it's sending in order to keep it straight and steady. If a clean recording is to be produced, a video-cassette recorder must store the sync pulses that are part of the video it is trying to record. This effort may not be noticeable if the device does not have genlock.
D. A television signal or video signal has three parts: the black-and-white portion, the color portion, and the synchronizing (sync) pulses. It's the sync pulses which keep the picture stable, which accompany it and keep it steady and straight. Whether it's a camera or a video-cassette recorder, each video source contains its own generator of these synchronizing pulses. To produce a clean recording, a video-cassette recorder must "lock-up" to the sync pulses that are part of the video it is trying to record. If the device does not have genlock, this effort may be very noticeable.

10._____

KEY (CORRECT ANSWERS)

1. C
2. B
3. A
4. B
5. D

6. A
7. B
8. D
9. C
10. D

PREPARING WRITTEN MATERIAL

EXAMINATION SECTION
TEST 1

DIRECTIONS: Each question consists of a sentence which may or may not be an example of good English usage. Examine each sentence, considering grammar, punctuation, spelling, capitalization, and awkwardness. Then choose the correct statement about it from the four choices below it. If the English usage in the sentence given is better than any of the changes suggested in choices B, C, or D, pick choice A. (Do not pick a choice that will change the meaning of the sentence.)

1. We attended a staff conference on Wednesday the new safety and fire rules were discussed.

    A. This is an example of acceptable writing.
    B. The words "safety," "fire" and "rules" should begin with capital letters.
    C. There should be a comma after the word "Wednesday."
    D. There should be a period after the word "Wednesday" and the word "the" should begin with a capital letter

2. Neither the dictionary or the telephone directory could be found in the office library.

    A. This is an example of acceptable writing.
    B. The word "or" should be changed to "nor."
    C. The word "library" should be spelled "libery."
    D. The word "neither" should be changed to "either."

3. The report would have been typed correctly if the typist could read the draft.

    A. This is an example of acceptable writing.
    B. The word "would" should be removed.
    C. The word "have" should be inserted after the word "could."
    D. The word "correctly" should be changed to "correct."

4. The supervisor brought the reports and forms to an employees desk.

    A. This is an example of acceptable writing.
    B. The word "brought" should be changed to "took."
    C. There should be a comma after the word "reports" and a comma after the word "forms."
    D. The word "employees" should be spelled "employee's."

5. It's important for all the office personnel to submit their vacation schedules on time.

    A. This is an example of acceptable writing.
    B. The word "It's" should be spelled "Its."
    C. The word "their" should be spelled "they're."
    D. The word "personnel" should be spelled "personal."

6. The report, along with the accompanying documents, were submitted for review. 6.____

   A. This is an example of acceptable writing.
   B. The words "were submitted" should be changed to "was submitted."
   C. The word "accompanying" should be spelled "accompaning."
   D. The comma after the word "report" should be taken out.

7. If others must use your files, be certain that they understand how the system works, but insist that you do all the filing and refiling. 7.____

   A. This is an example of acceptable writing.
   B. There should be a period after the word "works," and the word "but" should start a new sentence
   C. The words "filing" and "refiling" should be spelled "fileing" and "refileing."
   D. There should be a comma after the word "but."

8. The appeal was not considered because of its late arrival. 8.____

   A. This is an example of acceptable writing.
   B. The word "its" should be changed to "it's."
   C. The word "its" should be changed to "the."
   D. The words "late arrival" should be changed to "arrival late."

9. The letter must be read carefully to determine under which subject it should be filed. 9.____

   A. This is an example of acceptable writing.
   B. The word "under" should be changed to "at."
   C. The word "determine" should be spelled "determin."
   D. The word "carefuly" should be spelled "carefully."

10. He showed potential as an office manager, but he lacked skill in delegating work. 10.____

    A. This is an example of acceptable writing.
    B. The word "delegating" should be spelled "delagating."
    C. The word "potential" should be spelled "potencial."
    D. The words "he lacked" should be changed to "was lacking."

KEY (CORRECT ANSWERS)

1.	D	6.	B
2.	B	7.	A
3.	C	8.	A
4.	D	9.	D
5.	A	10.	A

TEST 2

DIRECTIONS: Each question consists of a sentence which may or may not be an example of good English usage. Examine each sentence, considering grammar, punctuation, spelling, capitalization, and awkwardness. Then choose the correct statement about it from the four choices below it. If the English usage in the sentence given is better than any of the changes suggested in choices B, C, or D, pick choice A. (Do not pick a choice that will change the meaning of the sentence.)

1. The supervisor wants that all staff members report to the office at 9:00 A.M.

    A. This is an example of acceptable writing.
    B. The word "that" should be removed and the word "to" should be inserted after the word "members."
    C. There should be a comma after the word "wants" and a comma after the word "office."
    D. The word "wants" should be changed to "want" and the word "shall" should be inserted after the word "members."

2. Every morning the clerk opens the office mail and distributes it.

    A. This is an example of acceptable writing.
    B. The word "opens" should be changed to "open."
    C. The word "mail" should be changed to "letters."
    D. The word "it" should be changed to "them."

3. The secretary typed more fast on a desktop computer than on a laptop computer.

    A. This is an example of acceptable writing.
    B. The words "more fast" should be changed to "faster."
    C. There should be a comma after the words "desktop computer."
    D. The word "than" should be changed to "then."

4. The new stenographer needed a desk a computer, a chair and a blotter.

    A. This is an example of acceptable writing.
    B. The word "blotter" should be spelled "blodder."
    C. The word "stenographer" should begin with a capital letter.
    D. There should be a comma after the word "desk."

5. The recruiting officer said, "There are many different goverment jobs available."

    A. This is an example of acceptable writing.
    B. The word "There" should not be capitalized.
    C. The word "goverment" should be spelled "government".
    D. The comma after the word "said" should be removed.

6. He can recommend a mechanic whose work is reliable.

    A. This is an example of acceptable writing.
    B. The word "reliable" should be spelled "relyable."
    C. The word "whose" should be spelled "who's."
    D. The word "mechanic" should be spelled "mecanic."

7. She typed quickly; like someone who had not a moment to lose. 7.____

    A. This is an example of acceptable writing.
    B. The word "not" should be removed.
    C. The semicolon should be changed to a comma.
    D. The word "quickly" should be placed before instead of after the word "typed."

8. She insisted that she had to much work to do. 8.____

    A. This is an example of acceptable writing.
    B. The word "insisted" should be spelled "incisted."
    C. The word "to" used in front of "much" should be spelled "too."
    D. The word "do" should be changed to "be done."

9. He excepted praise from his supervisor for a job well done. 9.____

    A. This is an example of acceptable writing.
    B. The word "excepted" should be spelled "accepted."
    C. The order of the words "well done" should be changed to "done well."
    D. There should be a comma after the word "supervisor."

10. What appears to be intentional errors in grammar occur several times in the passage. 10.____

    A. This is an example of acceptable writing.
    B. The word "occur" should be spelled "occurr."
    C. The word "appears" should be changed to "appear."
    D. The phrase "several times" should be changed to "from time to time."

KEY (CORRECT ANSWERS)

1.	B	6.	A
2.	A	7.	C
3.	B	8.	C
4.	D	9.	B
5.	C	10.	C

TEST 3

Questions 1-5.

DIRECTIONS: Same as for Tests 1 and 2.

1. The clerk could have completed the assignment on time if he knows where these materials were located.

    A. This is an example of acceptable writing.
    B. The word "knows" should be replaced by "had known."
    C. The word "were" should be replaced by "had been."
    D. The words "where these materials were located" should be replaced by "the location of these materials."

2. All employees should be given safety training. Not just those who have accidents.

    A. This is an example of acceptable writing.
    B. The period after the word "training" should be changed to a colon.
    C. The period after the word "training" should be changed to a semicolon, and the first letter of the word "Not" should be changed to a small "n."
    D. The period after the word "training" should be changed to a comma, and the first letter of the word "Not" should be changed to a small "n."

3. This proposal is designed to promote employee awareness of the suggestion program, to encourage employee participation in the program, and to increase the number of suggestions submitted.

    A. This is an example of acceptable writing.
    B. The word "proposal" should be spelled "preposal."
    C. The words "to increase the number of suggestions submitted" should be changed to "an increase in the number of suggestions is expected."
    D. The word "promote" should be changed to "enhance" and the word "increase" should be changed to "add to."

4. The introduction of inovative managerial techniques should be preceded by careful analysis of the specific circumstances and conditions in each department.

    A. This is an example of acceptable writing.
    B. The word "techniques" should be spelled "techneques."
    C. The word "inovative" should be spelled "innovative."
    D. A comma should be placed after the word "circumstances" and after the word "conditions."

5. This occurrence indicates that such criticism embarrasses him.

    A. This is an example of acceptable writing.
    B. The word "occurrence" should be spelled "occurence."
    C. The word "criticism" should be spelled "critisism."
    D. The word "embarrasses" should be spelled "embarasses."

KEY (CORRECT ANSWERS)

1. B
2. D
3. A
4. C
5. A

EXAMINATION SECTION
TEST 1

DIRECTIONS: Each question or incomplete statement is followed by several suggested answers or completions. Select the one that BEST answer the question or completes the statement. PRINT THE LETTER OF THE CORRECT ANSWER IN THE SPACE AT THE RIGHT.

1. Although some kinds of instructions are best put in written form, a supervisor can give many instructions verbally.
    In which one of the following situations would verbal instructions be MOST suitable?

    A. Furnishing an employee with the details to be checked in doing a certain job
    B. Instructing an employee on the changes necessary to update the office manual used in your unit
    C. Informing a new employee where different kinds of supplies and equipment that he might need are kept
    D. Presenting an assignment to an employee who will be held accountable for following a series of steps

2. You may be asked to evaluate the organization structure of your unit.
    Which one of the following questions would you NOT expect to take up in an evaluation of this kind?

    A. Is there an employee whose personal problems are interfering with his or her work?
    B. Is there an up-to-date job description for each position in this section?
    C. Are related operations and tasks grouped together and regularly assigned together?
    D. Are responsibilities divided as far as possible, and. is this division clearly understood by all employees?

3. In order to distribute and schedule work fairly and efficiently, a supervisor may wish to make a work distribution study. A simple way of getting the information necessary for such a study is to have everyone for one week keep track of each task done and the time spent on each.
    Which one of the following situations showing up in such a study would *most clearly* call for corrective action?

    A. The newest employee takes longer to do most tasks than do experienced employees
    B. One difficult operation takes longer to do than most other operations carried out by the section
    C. A particular employee is very frequently assigned tasks that are not similar and have no relationship to each other
    D. The most highly skilled employee is often assigned the most difficult jobs

4. The authority to carry out a job can be delegated to a subordinate, but the supervisor remains responsible for the work of the section as a whole.
    As a supervisor, which of the following rules would be the BEST one for you to follow in view of the above statement?

A. Avoid assigning important tasks to your subordinates, because you will be blamed if anything goes wrong
B. Be sure each subordinate understands the specific job he has been assigned, and check at intervals to make sure assignments are done properly
C. Assign several people to every important job, so that responsibility will be spread out as much as possible
D. Have an experienced subordinate check all work done by other employees, so that there will be little chance of anything going wrong

5. The human tendency to resist change is often reflected in higher rates of turnover, absenteeism, and errors whenever an important change is made in an organization. Although psychologists do not fully understand the reasons why people resist change, they believe that the resistance stems from a threat to the individual's security, that it is a form of fear of the unknown.
In light of this statement, which one of the following approaches would probably be *MOST* effective in preparing employees for a change in procedure in their unit?

A. Avoid letting employees know anything about the change until the last possible moment
B. Sympathize with employees who resent the change and let them know you share their doubts and fears
C. Promise the employees that if the change turns out to be a poor one, you will allow them to suggest a return to the old system
D. Make sure that employees know the reasons for the change and are aware of the benefits that are expected from it

6. Each of the following methods of encouraging employee participation in work planning has been used effectively with different kinds and sizes of employee groups.
Which one of the following methods would be *MOST* suitable for a group of four technically skilled employees?

A. Discussions between the supervisor and a representative of the group
B. A suggestion program with semi-annual awards for outstanding suggestions
C. A group discussion summoned whenever a major problem remains unsolved for more than a month
D. Day-to-day exchange of information, opinions and experience

7. Of the following, the *MOST* important reason why a supervisor is given the authority to tell subordinates what work they should do, how they should do it, and when it should be done is that *usually*

A. most people will not work unless there is someone with authority standing over them
B. work is accomplished more effectively if the supervisor plans and coordinates it
C. when division of work is left up to subordinates, there is constant arguing, and very little work is accomplished
D. subordinates are not familiar with the tasks to be performed

8. Fatigue is a factor that affects productivity in all work situations. However, a brief rest period will ordinarily serve to restore a person from fatigue.
According to this statement, which one of the following techniques is *most likely* to reduce the impact of fatigue on over-all productivity in a unit?

A. Scheduling several short breaks throughout the day
B. Allowing employees to go home early
C. Extending the lunch period an extra half hour
D. Rotating job assignments every few weeks

9. After giving a new task to an employee, it is a good idea for a supervisor to ask specific questions to make sure that the employee grasps the essentials of the task and sees how it can be carried out. Questions which ask the employee what he thinks or how he feels about an important aspect of the task are particularly effective.
Which one of the following questions is *NOT* the type of question which would be useful in the foregoing situation?

    A. "Do you feel there will be any trouble meeting the 4:30 deadline?"
    B. "How do you feel about the kind of work we do here?"
    C. "Do you think that combining those two steps will work all right?"
    D. "Can you think of any additional equipment you may need for this process?"

10. Of the following, the *LEAST* important reason for having a *continuous* training program is that

    A. employees may forget procedures that they have already learned
    B. employees may develop short cuts on the job that result in inaccurate work
    C. the job continues to change because of new procedures and equipment
    D. training is one means of measuring effectiveness and productivity on the job

11. In training a new employee, it is usually advisable to break down the job into meaningful parts and have the new employee master one part before going on to the next.
Of the following, the *BEST* reason for using this technique is to

    A. let the new employee know the reason for what he is doing and thus encourage him to remain in the unit
    B. make the employee aware of the importance of the work and encourage him to work harder
    C. show the employee that the work is easy so that he will be encouraged to work faster
    D. make it more likely that the employee will experience success and will be encouraged to continue learning the job

12. You may occasionally find a serious error in the work of one of your subordinates.
Of the following, the *BEST* time to discuss such an error with an employee *usually* is

    A. immediately after the error is found
    B. after about two weeks, since you will also be able to point out some good things that the employee has accomplished
    C. when you have discovered a pattern of errors on the part of this employee so that he will not be able to dispute your criticism
    D. after the error results in a complaint by your own supervisor

13. For very important announcements to the staff, a supervisor should usually use both written and oral communications. For example, when a new procedure is to be introduced, the supervisor can more easily obtain the group's acceptance by giving his subordinates a rough draft of the new procedure and calling a meeting of all his subordinates. The LEAST important benefit of this technique is that it will better enable the supervisor to

    A. explain why the change is necessary
    B. make adjustments in the new procedure to meet valid staff objections
    C. assign someone to carry out the new procedure
    D. answer questions about the new procedure

14. Assume that, while you are interviewing an individual to obtain information, the individual pauses in the middle of an answer.
    The BEST of the following actions for you to take at that time is to

    A. correct any inaccuracies in what he has said
    B. remain silent until he continues
    C. explain your position on the matter being discussed
    D. explain that time is short and that he must complete his story quickly

15. When you are interviewing someone to obtain information, the BEST of the following reasons for you to repeat certain of his exact words is to

    A. assure him that appropriate action will be taken
    B. encourage him to switch to another topic of discussion
    C. assure him that you agree with his point of view
    D. encourage him to elaborate on a point he has made

16. Generally, when writing a letter, the use of precise words and concise sentences is

    A. *good,* because less time will be required to write the letter
    B. *bad,* because it is most likely that the reader will think the letter is unimportant and will not respond favorably
    C. *good,* because it is likely that your desired meaning will be conveyed to the reader
    D. *bad,* because your letter will be too brief to provide adequate information

17. In which of the following cases would it be MOST desirable to have *two* cards for one individual in a *single* alphabetic file? The individual has

    A. a hyphenated surname
    B. two middle names
    C. a first name with an unusual spelling
    D. a compound first name

18. Of the following, it is MOST appropriate to use a form letter when it is necessary to answer many

    A. requests or inquiries from a single individual
    B. follow-up letters from individuals requesting additional information
    C. requests or inquiries about a single subject
    D. complaints from individuals that they have been unable to obtain various types of information

19. Assume that you are asked to make up a budget for your section for the coming year, and you are told that the most important function of the budget is its "control function." Of the following, "control" in this context implies, *most nearly,* that

    A. you will probably be asked to justify expenditures in any category when it looks as though these expenditures are departing greatly from the amount budgeted
    B. your section will probably not be allowed to spend more than the budgeted amount in any given category, although it is always permissible to spend less
    C. your section will be required to spend the exact amount budgeted in every category
    D. the budget will be filed in the Office of the Comptroller so that when the year is over the actual expenditures can be compared with the amounts in the budget

20. In writing a report, the practice of taking up the *least* important points *first* and the *most* important points *last* is a

    A. *good technique* since the final points made in a report will make the greatest impression on the reader
    B. *good technique* since the material is presented in a more logical manner and will lead directly to the conclusions
    C. *poor technique* since the reader's time is wasted by having to review irrelevant information before finishing the report
    D. *poor technique* since it may cause the reader to lose interest in the report and arrive at incorrect conclusions about the report

21. Typically, when the technique of "supervision by results" is practiced, higher management sets down, either implicitly or explicitly, certain performance standards or goals that the subordinate is expected to meet. So long as these standards are met, management interferes very little.
    The *most likely* result of the use of this technique is that it will

    A. lead to ambiguity in terms of goals
    B. be successful only to the extent that close direct supervision is practiced
    C. make it possible to evaluate both employee and supervisory effectiveness
    D. allow for complete dependence on the subordinate's part

22. When making written evaluations and reviews of the performance of subordinates, it is usually ADVISABLE to

    A. avoid informing the employee of the evaluation if it is critical because it may create hard feelings
    B. avoid informing the employee of the evaluation whether critical or favorable because it is tension-producing
    C. to permit the employee to see the evaluation but not to discuss it with him because the supervisor cannot be certain where the discussion might lead
    D. to discuss the evaluation openly with the employee because it helps the employee understand what is expected of him

23. There are a number of well-known and respected human relations principles that successful supervisors have been using for years in building good relationships with their employees. Which of the following does *NOT* illustrate such a principle?

A. Give clear and complete instructions
B. Let each person know how he is getting along
C. Keep an open-door policy
D. Make all relationships personal ones

24. Assume that it is necessary for you to give an unpleasant assignment to one of your subordinates. You expect this employee to raise some objections to this assignment.
The *most appropriate of* the following actions for you to take *FIRST* is to issue the assignment

   A. *orally*, with the further statement that you will not listen to any complaints
   B. *in writing*, to forestall any complaints by the employee
   C. *orally*, permitting the employee to express his feelings
   D. *in writing*, with a note that any comments should be submitted in writing

25. Suppose you have just announced at a staff meeting with your subordinates that a radical reorganization of work will take place next week. Your subordinates at the meeting appear to be excited, tense, and worried.
Of the following, the *BEST* action for you to take at that time is to

   A. schedule private conferences with each subordinate to obtain his reaction to the meeting
   B. close the meeting and tell your subordinates to return immediately to their work assignments
   C. give your subordinates some time to ask questions and discuss your announcement
   D. insist that your subordinates do not discuss your announcement among themselves or with other members of the agency

24. ____
25. ____

KEY (CORRECT ANSWERS)

1.	C	11.	D
2.	A	12.	A
3.	C	13.	C
4.	B	14.	B
5.	D	15.	D
6.	D	16.	C
7.	B	17.	A
8.	A	18.	C
9.	B	19.	A
10.	D	20.	D

21. C
22. D
23. D
24. C
25. C

TEST 2

DIRECTIONS: Each question or incomplete statement is followed by several suggested answers or completions. Select the one that BEST answer the question or completes the statement. PRINT THE LETTER OF THE CORRECT ANSWER IN THE SPACE AT THE RIGHT.

1. Of the following, the BEST way for a supervisor to increase employees' interest in their work is to

    A. allow them to make as many decisions as possible
    B. demonstrate to them that he is as technically competent as they
    C. give each employee a difficult assignment
    D. promptly convey to them instructions from higher manage-ment

    1.____

2. The one of the following which is LEAST important in maintaining a high level of productivity on the part of employees is the

    A. provision of optimum physical working conditions for employees
    B. strength of employees' aspirations for promotion
    C. anticipated satisfactions which employees hope to derive from their work
    D. employees' interest in their jobs

    2.____

3. Of the following, the MAJOR advantage of group problem-solving, as compared to individual problem-solving, is that groups will more readily

    A. abide by their own decisions
    B. agree with agency management
    C. devise new policies and procedures
    D. reach conclusions sooner

    3.____

4. The group problem-solving conference is a useful supervisory method for getting people to reach solutions to problems.
Of the following the reason that groups usually reach more realistic solutions than do individuals is that

    A. individuals, as a rule, take longer than do groups in reaching decisions and are therefore more likely to make an error
    B. bringing people together to let them confer impresses participants with the seriousness of problems
    C. groups are generally more concerned with the future in evaluating organizational problems
    D. the erroneous opinions of group members tend to be corrected by the other members

    4.____

5. A competent supervisor should be able to distinguish between human and technical problems.
Of the following, the MAJOR difference between such problems is that serious human problems, in comparison to ordinary technical problems,

    A. are remedied more quickly
    B. involve a lesser need for diagnosis
    C. are more difficult to define
    D. become known through indications which are usually the actual problem

    5.____

6. Of the following, the BEST justification for a public agency establishing an alcoholism program for its employees is that

   A. alcoholism has traditionally been looked upon with a certain amused tolerance by management and thereby ignored as a serious illness
   B. employees with drinking problems have twice as many on-the-job accidents, especially during the early years of the problem
   C. excessive use of alcohol is associated with personality instability hindering informal social relationships among peers and subordinates
   D. the agency's public reputation will suffer despite an employee's drinking problem being a personal matter of little public concern

7. Assume you are a manager and you find a group of maintenance employees assigned to your project drinking and playing cards for money in an incinerator room after their regular working hours.
   The one of the following actions it would be BEST for you to take is to

   A. suspend all employees immediately if there is no question in your mind as to the validity of the charges
   B. review the personnel records of those involved with the supervisor and make a joint decision on which employees should sustain penalties of loss of annual leave or fines
   C. ask the supervisor to interview each violator and submit written reports to you and thereafter consult with the supervisor about disciplinary actions
   D. deduct three days of annual leave from each employee involved if he pleads guilty in lieu of facing more serious charges

8. Assume that as a manager you must discipline a subordinate, but all of the pertinent facts necessary for a full determination of the appropriate disciplinary action to take are not yet available. However, you fear that a delay in disciplinary action may damage the morale of other employees.
   The one of the following which is MOST appropriate for you to do in this matter is to

   A. take immediate disciplinary action as if all the pertinent facts were available
   B. wait until all the pertinent facts are available before reaching a decision
   C. inform the subordinate that you know he is guilty, issue a stern warning, and then let him wait for your further action
   D. reduce the severity of the discipline appropriate for the violation

9. There are two standard dismissal procedures utilized by most public agencies. The first is the "open back door" policy, in which the decision of a supervisor in discharging an employee for reasons of inefficiency cannot be cancelled by the central personnel agency. The second is the "closed back door" policy, in which the central personnel agency can order the supervisor to restore the discharged employee to his position.
   Of the following, the major DISADVANTAGE of the "closed back door" policy as opposed to the "open back door" policy is that central personnel agencies are

   A. likely to approve the dismissal of employees when there is inadequate justification
   B. likely to revoke dismissal actions out of sympathy for employees
   C. less qualified than employing agencies to evaluate the efficiency of employees
   D. easily influenced by political, religious, and racial factors

10. The one of the following for which a formal grievance-handling system is LEAST useful is   10._____
    in

    A. reducing the frequency of employee complaints
    B. diminishing the likelihood of arbitrary action by supervisors
    C. providing an outlet for employee frustrations
    D. bringing employee problems to the attention of higher management

11. The one of the following managers whose leadership style involves the GREATEST del-   11._____
    egation of authority to subordinates is the one who presents to subordinates

    A. his ideas and invites questions
    B. his decision and persuades them to accept it
    C. the problem, gets their suggestions, and makes his decision
    D. a tentative decision which is subject to change

12. Which of the following is *most likely* to cause employee productivity standards to be set   12._____
    too high?

    A. Standards of productivity are set by first-line supervisors rather than by higher-level managers.
    B. Employees' opinions about productivity standards are sought through written questionnaires.
    C. Initial studies concerning productivity are conducted by staff specialists.
    D. Ideal work conditions assumed in the productivity standards are lacking in actual operations.

13. The one of the following which states the MAIN value of an organization chart for a man-   13._____
    ager is that such charts show the

    A. lines of formal authority
    B. manner in which duties are performed by each employee
    C. flow of work among employees on the same level
    D. specific responsibilities of each position

14. Which of the following BEST names the usual role of a line unit with regard to the organi-   14._____
    zation's programs?

    A. Seeking publicity   B. Developing
    C. Carrying out   D. Evaluating

15. Critics of promotion *from within* a public agency argue for hiring *from outside* the agency   15._____
    because they believe that promotion from within leads to

    A. resentment and consequent weakened morale on the part of those not promoted
    B. the perpetuation of outdated practices and policies
    C. a more complex hiring procedure than hiring from outside the agency
    D. problems of objectively appraising someone already in the organization

16. The one of the following management functions which *usually* can be handled MOST   16._____
    effectively by a committee is the

    A. settlement of interdepartmental disputes
    B. planning of routine work schedules
    C. dissemination of information
    D. assignment of personnel

17. Assume that you are serving on a committee which is considering proposals in order to recommend a new maintenance policy. After eliminating a number of proposals by unanimous consent, the committee is deadlocked on three proposals.
    The one of the following which is the BEST way for the committee to reach agreement on a proposal they could recommend is to

    A. consider and vote on each proposal separately by secret ballot
    B. examine and discuss the three proposals until the proponents of two of them are persuaded they are wrong
    C. reach a synthesis which incorporates the significant features of each proposal
    D. discuss the three proposals until the proponents of each one concede those aspects of the proposals about which there is disagreement

18. A commonly used training and development method for professional staff is the case method, which utilizes the description of a situation, real or simulated, to provide a common base for analysis, discussion, and problem-solving.
    Of the following, the MOST appropriate time to use the case method is when professional staff needs

    A. insight into their personality problems
    B. practice in applying management concepts to their own problems
    C. practical experience in the assignment of delegated responsibilities
    D. to know how to function in many different capacities

19. The incident process is a training and development method in which trainees are given a very brief statement of an event or of a situation presenting a job incident or an employee problem of special significance.
    Of the following, it is MOST appropriate to use the incident process when

    A. trainees need to learn to review and analyze facts before solving a problem
    B. there are a large number of trainees who require the same information
    C. there are too many trainees to carry on effective discussion
    D. trainees are not aware of the effect of their behavior on others

20. The one of the following types of information about which a new clerical employee is usually LEAST concerned during the orientation process is

    A. his specific job duties   B. where he will work
    C. his organization's history   D. who his associates will be

21. The one of the following which is the MOST important limitation on the degree to which work should be broken down into specialized tasks is the point at which

    A. there ceases to be sufficient work of a specialized nature to occupy employees
    B. training costs equal the half-yearly savings derived from further specialization
    C. supervision of employees performing specialized tasks becomes more technical than supervision of general employees
    D. it becomes more difficult to replace the specialist than to replace the generalist who performs a complex set of functions

22. When a supervisor is asked for his opinion of the suitability for promotion of a subordinate, the supervisor is actually being asked to predict the subordinate's future behavior in a new role.
Such a prediction is *most likely* to be accurate if the

   A. higher position is similar to the subordinate's current one
   B. higher position requires intangible personal qualities
   C. new position requires a high intellectual level of performance
   D. supervisor has had little personal association with the subordinate away from the job

23. In one form of the non-directive evaluation interview the supervisor communicates his evaluation to the employee and then listens to the employee's response without making further suggestions.
The one of the following which is the PRINCIPAL danger of this method of evaluation is that the employee is most likely to

   A. develop an indifferent attitude towards the supervisor
   B. fail to discover ways of improving his performance
   C. become resistant to change in the organization's structure
   D. place the blame for his shortcomings on his co-workers

24. In establishing rules for his subordinates, a superior should be PRIMARILY concerned with

   A. creating sufficient flexibility to allow for exceptions
   B. making employees aware of the reasons for the rules and the penalties for infractions
   C. establishing the strength of his own position in relation to his subordinates
   D. having his subordinates know that such rules will be imposed in a personal manner

25. The practice of conducting staff training sessions on a periodic basis is *generally* considered

   A. *poor;* it takes employees away from their work assignments
   B. *poor;* all staff training should be done on an individual basis
   C. *good;* it permits the regular introduction of new methods and techniques
   D. *good;* it ensures a high employee productivity rate

KEY (CORRECT ANSWERS)

1. A
2. A
3. A
4. D
5. C

6. B
7. C
8. B
9. C
10. A

11. C
12. D
13. A
14. C
15. B

16. A
17. C
18. B
19. A
20. C

21. A
22. A
23. B
24. B
25. C

SUPERVISION STUDY GUIDE

Social science has developed information about groups and leadership in general and supervisor-employee relationships in particular. Since organizational effectiveness is closely linked to the ability of supervisors to direct the activities of employees, these findings are important to executives everywhere.

IS A SUPERVISOR A LEADER?

First-line supervisors are found in all large business and government organizations. They are the men at the base of an organizational hierarchy. Decisions made by the head of the organization reach them through a network of intermediate positions. They are frequently referred to as part of the management team, but their duties seldom seem to support this description.

A supervisor of clerks, tax collectors, meat inspectors, or securities analysts is not charged with budget preparation. He cannot hire or fire the employees in his own unit on his say-so. He does not administer programs which require great planning, coordinating, or decision making.

Then what is he? He is the man who is directly in charge of a group of employees doing productive work for a business or government agency. If the work requires the use of machines, the men he supervises operate them. If the work requires the writing of reports, the men he supervises write them. He is expected to maintain a productive flow of work without creating problems which higher levels of management must solve. But is he a leader?

To carry out a specific part of an agency's mission, management creates a unit, staffs it with a group of employees and designates a supervisor to take charge of them. Management directs what this unit shall do, from time to time changes directions, and often indicates what the group should not do. Management presumably creates status for the supervisor by giving him more pay, a title, and special priviledges.

Management asks a supervisor to get his workers to attain organizational goals, including the desired quantity and quality of production. Supposedly, he has authority to enable him to achieve this objective. Management at least assumes that by establishing the status of the supervisor's position it has created sufficient authority to enable him to achieve these goals -- not his goals, nor necessarily the group's, but management's goals.

In addition, supervision includes writing reports, keeping records of membership in a higher-level administrative group, industrial engineering, safety engineering, editorial duties, housekeeping duties, etc. The supervisor as a member of an organizational network, must be responsible to the changing demands of the management above him. At the same time, he must be responsive to the demands of the work group of which he is a member. He is placed in the difficult position of communicating and implementing new decisions, changed programs and revised production quotas for his work group, although he may have had little part in developing them.

It follows, then, that supervision has a special characteristic: achievement of goals, previously set by management, through the efforts of others. It is in this feature of the supervisor's job that we find the role of a leader in the sense of the following definition: *A leader is that person who most effectively influences group activities toward goal setting and goal achievements.*

This definition is broad. It covers both leaders in groups that come together voluntarily and in those brought together through a work assignment in a factory, store, or government agency. In the natural group, the authority necessary to attain goals is determined by the group membership and is granted by them. In the working group, it is apparent that the establishment of a supervisory position creates a predisposition on the part of employees to accept the authority of the occupant of that position. We cannot, however, assume that mere occupancy confers authority sufficient to assure the accomplishment of an organization's goals.

Supervision is different, then, from leadership. The supervisor is expected to fulfill the role of leader but without obtaining a grant of authority from the group he supervises. The supervisor is expected to influence the group in the achieving of goals but is often handicapped by having little influence on the organizational process by which goals are set. The supervisor, because he works in an organizational setting, has the burdens of additional organizational duties and restrictions and requirements arising out of the fact that his position is subordinate to a hierarchy of higher-level supervisors. These differences between leadership and supervision are reflected in our definition: *Supervision is basically a leadership role, in a formal organization, which has as its objective the effective influencing of other employees.*

Even though these differences between supervision and leadership exist, a significant finding of experimenters in this field is that supervisors must be leaders to be successful.

The problem is: How can a supervisor exercise leadership in an organizational setting? We might say that the supervisor is expected to be a natural leader in a situation which does not come about naturally. His situation becomes really difficult in an organization which is more eager to make its supervisors into followers rather than leaders.

LEADERSHIP: NATURAL AND ORGANIZATIONAL

Leadership, in its usual sense of *natural* leadership, and supervision are not the same. In some cases, leadership embraces broader powers and functions than supervision; in other cases, supervision embraces more than leadership. This is true both because of the organization and technical aspects of the supervisor's job and because of the relatively freer setting and inherent authority of the natural leader.

The natural leader usually has much more authority and influence than the supervisor. Group members not only follow his command but prefer it that way. The employee, however, can appeal the supervisor's commands to his union or to the supervisor's superior or to the personnel office. These intercessors represent restrictions on the supervisor's power to lead.

The natural leader can gain greater membership involvement in the group's objectives, and he can change the objectives of the group. The supervisor can attempt to gain employee support only for management's objectives; he cannot set other objectives. In these instances leadership is broader than supervision.

The natural leader must depend upon whatever skills are available when seeking to attain objectives. The supervisor is trained in the administrative skills necessary to achieve management's goals. If he does not possess the requisite skills, however, he can call upon management's technicians.

A natural leader can maintain his leadership, in certain groups, merely by satisfying members' need for group affilation. The supervisor must maintain his leadership by directing and organizing his group to achieve specific organizational goals set for him and his group by management. He must have a technical competence and a kind of coordinating ability which is not needed by many natural leaders.

A natural leader is responsible only to his group which grants him authority. The supervisor is responsible to management, which employs him, and, also, to the work group of which he is a member. The supervisor has the exceedingly difficult job of reconciling the demands of two groups frequently in conflict. He is often placed in the untenable position of trying to play two antagonisic roles. In the above instances, supervision is broader than leadership.

ORGANIZATIONAL INFLUENCES ON LEADERSHIP

The supervisor is both a product and a prisoner of the organization wherein we find him. The organization which creates the supervisor's position also obstructs, restricts, and channelizes the exercise of his duties. These influences extend beyond prescribed functional relationships to specific supervisory behavior. For example, even in a face-to-face situation involving one of his subordinates, the supervisor's actions are controlled to a great extent by his organization. His behavior must conform to the organization policy on human relations, rules which dictate personnel procedures, specific prohibitions governing conduct, the attitudes of his own superior, etc. He is not a free agent operating within the limits of his work group. His freedom of action is much more circumscribed than is generally admitted. The organizational influences which limit his leadership actions can be classified as structure, prescriptions, and proscriptions.

The organizational structure places each supervisor's position in context with other designated positions. It determines the relationships between his position and specific positions which impinge on his. The structure of the organization designates a certain position to which he looks for orders and information about his work. It gives a particular status to his position within a pattern of statuses from which he perceives that (1) certain positions are on a par, organizationally, with his, (2) other positions are subordinate, and (3) still others are superior. The organizational structure determines those positions to which he should look for advice and assistance, and those positions to which he should give advice and assistance.

For instance, the organizational structure has predetermined that the supervisor of a clerical processing unit shall report to a supervisory position in a higher echelon. He shall have certain relationships with the supervisors of the work units which transmit work to and receive work from his unit. He shall discuss changes and clarification of procedures with certain staff units, such as organization and methods, cost accounting, and personnel. He shall consult supervisors of units which provide or receive special work assignments.

The organizational structure, however, establishes patterns other than those of the relationships of positions. These are the patterns of responsibility, authority, and expectations.

The supervisor is responsible for certain activities or results; he is presumably invested with the authority to achieve these. His set of authority and responsibility is interwoven with other sets to the end that all goals and functions of the organization are parceled out in small, manageable lots. This, of course, establishes a series of expectations: a single supervisor can perform his particular set of duties only upon the assumption that preceding or contiguous sets of duties have been, or are being, carried out. At the same time, he is aware of the expectations of others that he will fulfill his functional role.

The structure of an organization establishes relationships between specified positions and specific expectations for these positions. The fact that these relationships and expectations are established is one thing; whether or not they are met is another.

PRESCRIPTIONS AND PROSCRIPTIONS

But let us return to the organizational influences which act to restrict the supervisor's exercise of leadership. These are the prescriptions and proscriptions generally in effect in all organizations, and those peculiar to a single organization. In brief these are the *thous shalt's* and the *thou shalt not's*.

Organizations not only prescribe certain duties for individual supervisory positions, they also prescribe specific methods and means of carrying out these duties and maintaining management-employee relations. These include rules, regulations, policy, and. tradition. It does no good for the supervisor to say, *This seems to be the best way to handle such-and such,* if the organization has established a routine for dealing with problems. For good or bad, there are rules that state that firings shall be executed in such a manner, accompanied by a certain notification; that training shall be conducted, and in this manner. Proscriptions are merely negative prescriptions: you may not discriminate against any employee because of politics or race; you shall not suspend any employee without following certain procedures and obtaining certain approvals.

Most of these prohibitions and rules apply to the area of interpersonal relations, precisely the area which is now arousing most interest on the part of administrators and managers. We have become concerned about the contrast between formally prescribed relationships and interpersonal relationships, and this brings us to the often discussed informal organization.

FORMAL AND INFORMAL ORGANIZATIONS

As we well know, the functions and activities of any organization are broken down into individual units of work called positions. Administrators must establish a pattern which will link these positions to each other and relate them to a system of authority and responsibility. Man-to-man are spelled out as plainly as possible for all to understand. Managers, then, build an official structure which we call the formal organization.

In these same organizations employees react individually and in groups to institutionally determined roles. John, a worker, rides in the same car pool as Joe, a foreman. An unplanned communication develops. Harry, a machinist, knows more about highspeed machining than his foreman or anyone else in his shop. An unofficial tool boss comes into being. Mary, who fought with Jane is promoted over her. Jane now ignores Mary's directions. A planned relationship fails to develop. The employees have built a structure which we call the informal organization.

> *Formal organization is a system of management-prescribed relations between positions in an organization.*
>
> *Informal organization is a network of unofficial relations between people in an organization.*

These definitions might lead us to the absurd conclusion that positions carry out formal activities and that employees spend their time in unofficial activities. We must recognize that organizational activities are in all cases carried out by people. The formal structure provides a needed framework within which interpersonal relations occur. What we call informal organization is the complex of normal, natural relations among employees. These personal relationships may be negative or positive. That is, they may impede or aid the achievement of organizational, goals. For example, friendship between two supervisors greatly increases the probability of good cooperation and coordination between their sections. On the other hand, *buck passing* nullifies the formal structure by failure to meet a prescribed and expected responsibility.

It is improbable that an ideal organization exists where all activities are acarried out in strict conformity to a formally prescribed pattern of functional roles. Informal organization arises because of the incompleteness and ambiguities in the network of formally prescribed relationships, or in response to the needs or inadequacies of supervisors or managers who hold prescribed functional roles in an organization. Many of these relationships are not prescribed by the organizational pattern; many cannot be prescribed; many should not be prescribed.

Management faces the problem of keeping the informal organization in harmony with the mission of the agency. One way to do this is to make sure that all employees have a clear understanding of and are sympathetic with that mission. The issuance of organizational charts, procedural manuals, and functional descriptions of the work to be done by divisions and sections helps communicate management's plans and goals. Issuances alone, of course, cannot do the whole job. They should be accompanied by oral discussion and explanation. Management must ensure that there is mutual understanding and acceptance of charts and procedures. More important is that management acquaint itself with the attitudes, activities, and peculiar brands of logic which govern the informal organization. Only through this type of knowledge can they and supervisors keep informal goals consistent with the agency mission.

SUPERVISION, STATUS, AND FUNCTIONAL ROLE

A well-established supervisor is respected by the employees who work with him. They defer to his wishes. It is clear that a superior-subordinate relationship has been established. That is, status of the supervisor has been established in relation to other employees of the same work group. This same supervisor gains the respect of employees when he behaves in a certain manner. He will be expected generally, to follow the customs of the group in such matters as dress, recreation, and manner of speaking. The group has a set of expectations as to his behavior. His position is a functional role which carries with it a collection of rights and obligations.

The position of supervisor usually has a status distinct from the individual who occupies it: it is much like a position description which exists whether or not there is an incumbent. The status of a supervisory position is valued higher than that of an employee position both because of the functional role of leadership which is assigned to it and because of the status symbols of titles, rights, and privileges which go with it.

Social ranking, or status, is not simple because it involves both the position and the man. An individual may be ranked higher than others because of his education, social background, perceived leadership ability, or conformity to group customs and ideals. If such a man is ranked higher by the members of a work group than their supervisor, the supervisor's effectiveness may be seriously undermined.

If the organization does not build and reinforce a supervisor's status, his position can be undermined in a different way. This will happen when managers go around rather than through the supervisor or designate him as a straw boss, acting boss, or otherwise not a real boss.

Let us clarify this last point. A role, and corresponding status, establishes a set of expectations. Employees expect their supervisor to do certain things and to act in certain ways. They are prepared to respond to that expected behavior. When the supervisor's behavior does not conform to their expectations, they are surprised, confused, and ill-at-ease. It becomes necessary for them to resolve their confusion, if they can. They might do this by turning to one of their own members for leadership. If the confusion continues, or their attempted solutions are not satisfactory, they will probably become a poorly motivated, non-cohesive group which cannot function very well.

COMMUNICATION AND THE SUPERVISOR

In a recent survey railroad workers reported that they rarely look to their supervisors for information about the company. This is startling, at least to us, because we ordinarily think of the supervisor as the link between management and worker. We expect the supervisor to be the prime source of information about the company. Actually, the railroad workers listed the supervisor next to last in the order of their sources of information. Most suprising of all, the supervisors, themselves, stated that rumor and unofficial contacts were their principal sources of information. Here we see one of the reasons why supervisors may not be as effective as management desires.

The supervisor is not only being bypassed by his work group, he is being ignored, and his position weakened, by the very organization which is holding him responsible for the activities of his workers. If he is management's representative to the employee, then management has an obligation to keep him informed of its activities. This is necessary if he is to carry out his functions efficiently and maintain his leadership in the work group. The supervisor is expected to be a source of information; when he is not, his status is not clear, and employees are dissatisfied because he has not lived up to expectations.

By providing information to the supervisor to pass along to employees, we can strengthen his position as leader of the group, and increase satisfaction and cohesion within the group. Because he has more information than the other members, receives information sooner, and passes it along at the proper times, members turn to him as a source and also provide him with information in the hope of receiving some in return. From this we can see an increase in group cohesiveness because:

- Employees are bound closer to their supervisor because he is *in the know*
- there is less need to go outside the group for answers
- employees will more quickly turn to the supervisor for enlightenment.

The fact that he has the answers will also enhance the supervisor's standing in the eyes of his men. This increased sta,tus will serve to bolster his authority and control of the group and will probably result in improved morale and productivity.

The foregoing, of course, does not mean that all management information should be given out. There are obviously certain policy determinations and discussions which need not or cannot be transmitted to all supervisors. However, the supervisor must be kept as fully informed as possible so that he can answer questions when asked and can allay needless fears and anxieties. Further, the supervisor has the responsibility of encouraging employee questions and submissions of information. He must be able to present information to employees so that it is clearly understood and accepted. His attitude and manner should make it clear that he believes in what he is saying, that the information is necessary or desirable to the group, and that he is prepared to act on the basis of the information.

SUPERVISION AND JOB PERFORMANCE

The productivity of work groups is a product; employees' efforts are multiplied by the supervision they receive. Many investigators have analyzed this relationship and have discovered elements of supervision which differentiate high and low production groups. These researchers have identified certain types of supervisory practices which they classify as *employee-centered* and other types which they classify as *production centered*.

The difference between these two kinds of supervision lies not in specific practices but in the approach or orientation to supervision. The employee-centered supervisor directs most of his efforts toward increasing employee motivation. He is concerned more with realizing the potential energy of persons than with administrative and technological methods of increasing efficiency and productivity. He is the man who finds ways of causing employees to want to work harder with the same tools. These supervisors emphasize the personal relations between their employees and themselves.

Now, obviously, these pictures are overdrawn. No one supervisor has all the virtues of the ideal type of employee-centered supervisor. And, fortunately, no one supervisor has all the bad traits found in many production-centered supervisors. We should remember that the various practices that researchers have found which distinguish these two kinds of supervision represent the many practices and methods of supervisors of all gradations between these extremes. We should be careful, too, of the implications of the labels attached to the two types. For instance, being production-centered is not necessarily bad, since the principal responsibility of any supervisor is maintaining the production level that is expected of his work group. Being employee-centered may not necessarily be good, if the only result is a happy, chuckling crew of loafers. To return to the researchers's findings, employee-centered supervisors:

- Recommend promotions, transfers, pay increases
- Inform men about what is happening in the company
- Keep men posted on how well they are doing
- Hear complaints and grievances sympathetically
- Speak up for subordinates

Production-centered supervisors, on the other hand, don't do those things. They check on employees more frequently, give more detailed and frequent instructions, don't give reasons for changes, and are more punitive when mistakes are made. Employee-centered supervisors were reported to contribute to high morale and high production, whereas production-centered supervision was associated with lower morale and less production.

More recent findings, however, show that the relationship between supervision and productivity is not this simple. Investigators now report that high production is more frequently associated with supervisory practices which combine employee-centered behavior with concern for production. (This concern is not the same, however, as anxiety about production, which is the hallmark of our production-centered supervisor.) Let us examine these apparently contradictory findings and the premises from which they are derived.

SUPERVISION AND MORALE

Why do supervisory activities cause high or low production? As the name implies, the activities of the employee-centered supervisor tend to relate him more closely and satisfactorily to his workers. The production-centered supervisor's practices tend to separate him from his group and to foster antagonism. An analysis of this difference may answer our question.

Earlier, we pointed out that the supervisor is a type of leader and that leadership is intimately related to the group in which it occurs. We discover, now, that an employee-centered supervisor's primary activities are concerned with both his leadership and his group membership. Such a supervisor is a member of a group and occupies a leadership role in that group.

These facts are sometimes obscured when we speak of the supervisor as management's representative, or as the organizational link between management and the employee, or as the end of the chain of command. If we really want to understand what it is we expect of the supervisor, we must remember that he is the designated leader of a group of employees to whom he is bound by interaction and interdependence.

Most of his actions are aimed, consciously or unconsciously, at strengthening membership ties in the group. This includes both making members more conscious that he is a member of their grout) and causing members to identify themselves more closely with the group. These ends are accomplished by:

    making the group more attractive to the worker: they
        find satisfaction of their needs for recognition,
        friendship, enjoyable work, etc.;

    maintaining open communication: employees can express
        their views and obtain information about the organization.

    giving assistance: members can seek advice on
        personal problems as well as their work; and
    acting as a buffer between the group and management:
        he speaks up for his men and explains the reasons
        for management's decisions.

Such actions both strengthen group cohesiveness and solidarity and affirm the supervisor's leadership position in the group.

DEFINING MORALE

This brings us back to a point mentioned earlier. We had said that employee-centered supervisors contribute to high morale as well as to high production. But how can we explain units which have low morale and high productivity, or vice versa? Usually production and morale are considered separately, partly because they are measured against different criteria and partly because, in some instances, they seem to be independent of each other.

Some of this difficulty may stem from confusion over definitions of morale. Morale has been defined as, or measured by, absences from work, satisfaction with job or company, dissension among members of work groups, productivity, apathy or lack of interest, readiness to help others, and a general aura of happiness as rated by observers. Some of these criteria of morale are not subject to the influence of the supervisor, and some of them are not clearly related to productivity. Definitions like these invite findings of low morale coupled with high production.

Both productivity and morale can be influenced by environmental factors not under the control of group members or supervisors. Such things as plant layout, organizational structure and goals, lighting, ventilation, communications, and management planning may have an adverse or desirable effect.

We might resolve the dilemma by defining morale on the basis of our understanding of the supervisor as leader of a group; morale is the degree of satisfaction of group members with their leadership. In this light, the supervisor's employee-centered activities bear a clear relation to morale. His efforts to increase employee identification with the group and to strengthen his leadership lead to greater satisfaction with that leadership. By increasing group cohesiveness and by demonstrating that his influence and power can aid the group, he is able to enhance his leadership status and afford satisfaction to the group.

SUPERVISION, PRODUCTION, AND MORALE

There are factors within the organization itself which determine whether increased production is possible:

Are production goals expressed in terms understandable to employees and are they realistic?

Do supervisors responsible for production respect the agency mission and production goals?

If employees do not know how to do the job well, does management provide a trainer--often the supervisor--who can teach efficient work methods?

There are other factors within the work group which determine whether increased production will be attained:

Is leadership present which can bring about the desired level of production?

Are production goals accepted by employees as reasonable and attainable?

If group effort is involved, are members able to coordinate their efforts?

Research findings confirm the view that an employee-centered supervisor can achieve higher morale than a production-centered supervisor. Managers may well ask what is the relationship between this and production?

Supervision is production-oriented to the extent that it focuses attention on achieving organizational goals, and plans and devises methods for attaining them; it is employee-centered to the extent that it focuses attention on employee attitudes toward those goals, and plans and works toward maintenance of employee satisfaction.

High productivity and low morale result when a supervisor plans and organizes work efficiently but cannot achieve high membership satisfaction. Low production and high morale result when a supervisor, though keeping members satisfied with his leadership, either has not gained acceptance of organizational goals or does not have the technical competence to achieve them.

The relationship between supervision, morale, and productivity is an interdependent one, with the supervisor playing an integrating role due to his ability to influence productivity and morale independently of each other.

A supervisor who can plan his work well has good technical knowledge, and who can install better production methods can raise production without necessarily increasing group satisfaction. On the other hand, a supervisor who can motivate his employees and keep them satisfied with his leadership can gain high production in spite of technical difficulties and environmental obstacles.

CLIMATE AND SUPERVISION

Climate, the intangible environment of an organization made up of attitudes, beliefs, and traditions, plays a large part in morale, productivity, and supervision. Usually when we speak of climate and its relationship to morale and productivity, we talk about the merits of *democratic* versus *authoritarian* climate. Employees seem to produce more and have higher morale in a democratic climate, whereas in an authoritarian climate, the reverse seems to be true or so the researchers tell us. We would do well to determine what these terms mean to supervision.

Perhaps most of our difficulty in understanding and applying these concepts comes from our emotional reactions to the words themselves. For example, authoritarian climate is usually painted as the very blackest kind of dictatorship. This not surprising, because we are usually expected to believe that it is invariably bad. Conversely, democratic climate is drawn to make the driven snow look impure by comparison.

Now these descriptions are most probably true when we talk about our political processes, or town meetings, or freedom of speech. However the same labels have been used by social scientists in other contexts and have also been applied to government and business organizations, without, it seems, any recognition that the meanings and their social values may have changed somewhat .

For example, these labels were used in experiments conducted in an informal class room setting using 11 year old boys as subjects. The descriptive labels applied to the climate of the setting as well as the type of leadership practiced. When these labels were transferred to a management setting it seems that many presumed that they principally meant the king of leadership rather than climate. We can see that there is a great difference between the experimental and management settings and that leadership practices for one might be inappropriate for the other.

It is doubtful that formal work organizations can be anything but authoritarian, in that goals are set by management and a hierarchy exists through which decisions and orders from the top are transmitted downward. Organizations are authoritarian by structure and need: direction and control are placed in the hands of a few in order to gain fast and efficient decision making. Now this does not mean to describe a dictatorship. It is merely the recognition of the fact that direction of organizational affairs comes from above. It should be noted that leadership in some natural groups is, in this sense, authoritarian.

Granting that formal organizations have this kind of authoritarian leadership, can there be a democratic climate? Certainly there can be, but we would want to define and delimit this term. A more realistic meaning of democratic climate in organizations is, the use of permissive and participatory methods in management-employee relations. That is, a mutual exchange of information and explanation with the granting of individual freedom within certain restricted and defined limits. However, it is not our purpose to debate the merits of authoritarianism versus democracy. We recognize that within the small work group there is a need for freedom from constraint and an increase in participation in order to achieve organizational goals within the framework of the organizational environment.

Another aspect of climate is best expressed by this familiar, and true saying: actions speak louder than words. Of particular concern to us is this effect of management climate on the behavior of supervisors, particularly in employee-centered activities.

There have been reports of disappointment with efforts to make supervisors more employee-centered. Managers state that, since research has shown ways of improving human relations, supervisors should begin to practice these methods. Usually a training course in human relations is established, and supervisors are given this training. Managers then sit back and wait for the expected improvements, only to find that there are none.

If we wish to produce changes in the supervisor's behavior, the climate must be made appropriate and rewarding to the changed behavior. This means that top-level attitudes and behavior cannot deny or contradict the change we are attempting to effect. Basic changes in organizational behavior cannot be made with any permanence, unless we provide an environment that is receptive to the changes and rewards those persons who do change.

IMPROVING SUPERVISION

Anyone who has read this far might expect to find *A Dozen Rules for Dealing With Employees* or *29 Steps to Supervisory Success.* We will not provide such a list.

Simple rules suffer from their simplicity. They ignore the complexities of human behavior. Reliance upon rules may cause supervisors to concentrate on superficial aspects of their relations with employees. It may preclude genuine understanding.

The supervisor who relies on a list of rules tends to think of people in mechanistic terms. In a certain situation, he uses *Rule No. 3*. Employees are not treated as thinking and feeling persons, but rather as figures in a formula: Rule 3 applied to employee X = Production.

Employees usually recognize mechanical manipulation and become dissatisfied and resentful. They lose faith in, and respect for, their supervisor, and this may be reflected in lower morale and productivity.

We do not mean that supervisors must become social science experts if they wish to improve. Reports of current research indicate that there are two major parts of their job which can be strengthened through self-improvement: (1) Work planning, including technical skills. (2) Motivation of employees.

The most effective supervisors combine excellence in the administrative and technical aspects of their work with friendly and considerate personal relations with their employees.

CRITICAL PERSONAL RELATIONS

Later in this chaper we shall talk about administrative aspects of supervision, but first let us comment on *friendly and considerate personal relations*. We have discussed this subject throughout the preceding chapters, but we want to review some of the critical supervisory influences on personal relations.

Closeness of Supervision

The closeness of supervision has an important effect on productivity and morale. Mann and Dent found that supervisors of low-producing units supervise very closely, while high-producing supervisors exercise only general supervision. It was found that the low-producing supervisors:

- check on employees more frequently
- give more detailed and frequent instructions
- limit employee's freedom to do job in own way.

Workers who felt less closely supervised reported that they were better satisfied with their jobs and the company. We should note that the manner or attitude of the supervisor has an important bearing on whether employees perceive supervision as being close or general.

These findings are another way of saying that supervision does not mean standing over the employee and telling him what to do and when and how to do it. The more effective supervisor tells his employees what is required, giving general instructions.

COMMUNICATION

Supervisors of high-production units consider communication as one of the most important aspects of their job. Effective communication is used by these supervisors to achieve better interpersonal relations and improved employee motivation. Low-production supervisors do not rate communication as highly important.

High-producing supervisors find that an important aid to more effective communication is listening. They are ready to listen to both personal problems or interests and questions about the work. This does not mean that they are *nosey* or meddle in their employees' personal lives, but rather that they show a willingness to listen, and do listen, if their employees wish to discuss problems.

These supervisors inform employees about forthcoming changes in work; they discuss agency policy with employees; and they make sure that each employee knows how well he is doing. What these supervisors do is use two-way communication effectively. Unless the supervisor freely imparts information, he will not receive information in return.

Attitudes and perception are frequently affected by communication or the lack of it. Research surveys reveal that many supervisors are not aware of their employees' attitudes, nor do they know what personal reactions their supervision arouses. Through frank discussions with employees, they have been surprised to discover employee beliefs about which they were ignorant. Discussion sometimes reveals that the supervisor and his employees have totally different impressions about the same event. The supervisor should be constantly on the alert for misconceptions about his words and deeds. He must remember that, although his actions are perfectly clear to himself, they may be, and frequently are, viewed differently by employees.

Failure to communicate information results in misconceptions and false assumptions. What you say and how you say it will strongly affect your employees' attitudes and perceptions. By giving them available information you can prevent misconceptions; by discussion, you may be able to change attitudes; by questioning; you can discover what the perceptions and assumptions really are. And it need hardly be added that actions should conform very closely to words.

If we were to attempt to reduce the above discussion on communication to rules, we would have a long list which would be based on one cardinal principle: Don't make assumptions!

- o Don't assume that your employees know; tell them.
- o Don't assume that you know how they feel; find out.
- o Don't assume that they understand; clarify.

20 SUPERVISORY HINTS

1. Avoid inconsistency.
2. Always give employees a chance to explain their actions before taking disciplinary action. Don't allow too much time for a "cooling off" period before disciplining an employee.
3. Be specific in your criticisms.
4. Delegate responsibility wisely.
5. Do not argue or lose your temper, and avoid being impatient.
6. Promote mutual respect and be fair, impartial and open-minded.
7. Keep in mind that asking for employees' advice and input can be helpful in decision making.
8. If you make promises, keep them.
9. Always keep the feelings, abilities, dignity and motives of your staff in mind.
10. Remain loyal to your employees' interests.
11. Never criticize employees in front of others, or treat employees like children.
12. Admit mistakes. Don't place blame on your employees, or make excuses.
13. Be reasonable in your expectations, give complete instructions, and establish well-planned goals.
14. Be knowledgeable about office details and procedures, but avoid becoming bogged down in details.
15. Avoid supervising too closely or too loosely. Employees should also view you as an approachable supervisor.
16. Remember that employees' personal problems may affect job performance, but become involved only when appropriate.
17. Work to develop workers, and to instill a feeling of cooperation while working toward mutual goals.
18. Do not overpraise or underpraise, be properly appreciative.
19. Never ask an employee to discipline someone for you.
20. A complaint, even if unjustified, should be taken seriously.

BASIC FUNDAMENTALS OF VITAMINS

I. WHAT ARE VITAMINS?

They are a group of organic (carbon-containing) compounds that regulate reactions occurring in metabolism—the process by which the body breaks down and uses foods. Once called accessory food factors, vitamins are necessary because, just as water needs heat to boil, certain processes in the body won't occur properly without vitamins. Scientists don't fully understand why. The most popular theory is that the vitamins serve as traffic controllers, telling the body when certain procedures may begin, or determining speed and duration. Thus, the absence of a vitamin may block a reaction in a cell, thereby disrupting the cell's balance and causing it to form improperly or function abnormally.

Unlike some other organisms, the human body does not manufacture vitamins, and needs to acquire them from diet. Scientists now think that the reason is built in, a result of evolution. In the beginning, the theory goes, simple organisms could get everything they needed straight from the environment. But as life forms became more complex, the ability to make those compounds directly from elements in nature was lost. And in the case of vitamin C, they think that our body's inability to synthesize it is a form of *genetic disease*. That is, we did not discard the ability on the way to becoming *man*, but rather something went wrong in the formation of our metabolic process so that the ingredients we need to make vitamin C are completely missing.

Vitamins are subdivided into two basic classifications—water-soluble and fat-soluble.

Water-soluble vitamins (except vitamin C) serve as catalysts in metabolic activity. They help the body transfer energy from food, and aid in breaking down fats, carbohydrates, and proteins. During digestion, those vitamins are absorbed into the intestine - where no chemical reaction is needed to make them usable - and then pass directly to the bloodstream, where they are carried to body tissues for use. Each of the water-soluble vitamins serves a very special function in the body. For example, vitamins B_1 and B_6 control the conversion of carbohydrates and proteins into metabolic energy (calories), while niacin and riboflavin transport hydrogen during metabolism, thereby causing specific proteins, fats, and carbohydrates to be formed. Vitamin C aids in the formation of collagen, the connective tissue of skin, tendons, and bone, and in absorption and use of iron and potassium. Water-soluble vitamins are not normally stored in the body.

The fat-soluble vitamins are a much more sophisticated group. They serve more highly specialized functions and are much more selectively distributed in nature. They include vitamins A, D, E, and K, all of which can be stored in the body and can be toxic when taken in excess. The fat-solubles are necessary for the synthesis of some body enzymes (substances that speed up or start chemical reactions in the body), and form part of many biological membranes. They are transported by lymph from the intestines to the circulating blood. More fat-solubles than water-solubles are stored in the body, with A, D, and K stored in the liver and vitamin E stored in body fat. Also, since fat is necessary to break down those vitamins, anything that impedes fat metabolism can inhibit their use.

One of the best ways to make sure that your diet is providing your body with what it needs is to make sure that it is varied. It doesn't really matter if you do not savor a few members of any of the basic food groups, since there are enough other foods rich in the same nutrients to take up the slack. You don't have to eat liver to get iron, if you dislike it. Eat spinach in a salad instead and get plenty of iron and some vitamin A too.

Contrary to the faddist notion, the idea of taking each little vitamin in a separate tablet (as opposed to the more common multiple-vitamin tablet) is wrong. What people are doing by this practice is spending a good deal of money and taking the chance of vitamin overdose. It is simply useless to load the body with substances it can't possibly utilize.

In fact, the whole idea of vitamin pills is superfluous unless a person (1) has an illness that eliminates an entire food group from the diet, (2) is the sort of vegetarian who eschews eggs, butter, milk, cheese, and all meats, poultry, and fish, or (3) is pregnant, sick or so poor that a varied, quality diet is impossible. If you are in doubt about your supply of vitamins, ask your physician for advice and take only those prescribed.

Also, people should interpret in a common-sense way the *recommended daily requirement* phrase. This simply refers to an optimum amount that scientists have found to be healthy for humans. One will find that the United States requires one amount, Canada another, and some other country another. This doesn't at all mean that, if you're getting less than this amount of a vitamin, you're deficient.

II. FAT-SOLUBLE VITAMINS

Vitamin	Uses	Possible Results of Deficiency	Possible Results of Surplus	Sources
A (Retinol)	Serves in the formation of normal skin and the mucosa, internal skin, bone, and tooth formation, night and color vision	Deterioration of skin, faulty bone and tooth development, deterioration of eyes, night blindness and blindness	Drying and peeling of skin, loss of hair, bone, and joint pain, fragile bones, enlarged liver and spleen; in severe cases, death	Liver, butter, and fortified margarine, cream, whole milk and cheese made from whole milk, carrots, and dark green leafy vegetables
D	Regulates intestinal absorption of calcium and phosphorus and utilization of those minerals in bones and soft tissue, and plays a part in protein metabolism	In children: delayed tooth development, large joints, soft bones that are easily deformed and broken, deformities of chest, skull, spine, and pelvis (rickets). In adults: osteo-malacia (adult rickets), characterized by softening of bones	Weakness, weight loss, vomiting, diarrhea, calcium deposits in soft tissues, kidney damage and death	Formed by direct exposure of skin to sunlight, fortified milk, fish liver oils; also, small amounts of butter made in the summer, liver, egg yolk, and fatty fish like sardines, salmon, and tuna

Vitamin	Uses	Possible Results of Deficiency	Possible Results of Surplus	Sources
E	An antioxidant to reduce oxidation of vitamin A, the carotenes, and polyunsaturated fatty acids	Deficiency (rare and even difficult to produce experimentally) causes mild anemia and destruction of red blood cells	Excess (although there is no conclusive evidence) is believed to cause muscle damage and fatigue	Vegetable oils like cottonseed, safflower, sunflower, soybean; corn, almonds, peanuts, wheat germ, rice germ, asparagus, green leafy vegetables, liver, margarine, vegetable shortening
K	Necessary for proper clotting of blood	Leads to prolonged clotting time and hemorrhagic disease in newborn infants	Excess of menaquinone, a synthetic form, can cause jaundice in newborn infants, but natural forms have not been found to be toxic. An excess in adults is unlikely.	The main source is synthesis by normal bacteria in the intestine, a function that can be inhibited by some antibiotics. Food sources include lettuce, spinach, kale, cauliflower, cabbage, liver, egg yolk, soybean oils.

III. WATER-SOLUBLE VITAMINS

Vitamin	Uses	Possible Results of Deficiency	Possible Results of Surplus	Sources
C (Ascorbic Acid)	Aids in the formation of collagen, the connective tissue of skin, tendons, and bone, in the formation of hemoglobin, the absorption and use of iron and phosphorus, and possibly in the metabolism of protein and carbohydrates.	Poor bone and tooth development, bleeding gums, weakened cartilage and capillary walls, skin hemorrhages, anemia (scurvy)	A possible factor in the destruction of vitamin B_{12} in ingested food.	Citrus fruits, tomatoes, cantaloupe, and other melons, berries, green leafy vegetables, peppers, broccoli, cauliflower, and fresh potatoes

Vitamin	Uses	Possible Results of Deficiency	Possible Results of Surplus	Sources
B_1 (Thiamine)	Necessary for carbohydrate metabolism	Apathy, depression, poor appetite, lack of tone in the gastrointestinal tract, constipation, heart failure (beriberi)	No known effects	Whole-grain flours and cereals, wheat germ, seeds like sunflower and sesame, nuts like peanuts and pine nuts, legumes like soybeans, organ meats, pork (one of the richest sources) and leafy vegetables
B_2 (Riboflavin)	Used in enzymes that transport hydrogen in the body as part of the metabolism of carbohydrates, fats, and proteins	Cracks at corners of lips, scaly skin around nose and ears, sore tongue and mouth, itching, burning eyes, sensitivity to light	No known effects	Liver, kidney, cheese, milk, eggs, leafy vegetables, enriched bread, lean meat, beans, and peas
Niacin	Forms part of co-enzymes needed for hydrogen transport and for health of tissue cells	Skin rash, sore mouth and tongue, inflamed membranes in the digestive tract, depression, mental disorientation and stupor (pellagra)	Flushing of skin and occasionally jaundice	Organ meats, lean meats, poultry, fish, wheat germ and whole-grain flours and cereals, nuts, seeds, rice, beans, and peas. The amino acid tryptophan can be converted to niacin in the body
B_6	Used in metabolism of protein, essential for conversion of the amino acid tryptophan to niacin in the body	Dermatitis around eyes, at angles of mouth, sore mouth and smooth red tongue, weight loss, dizziness, vomiting, anemia, kidney stones, nervous disturbances and convulsions	No known effects	Seeds like sunflower, wheat germ and bran, whole-grain bread, flours and cereals, liver, meats, fish and poultry, potatoes, beans and brown rice

Vitamin	Uses	Possible Results of Deficiency	Possible Results of Surplus	Sources
Pantothenic acid	Essential to many chemical reactions, particularly metabolism and release of energy from fat, protein, and carbohydrates	Unlikely unless a part of total B vitamin deficiency. Unless the diet consists solely of highly processed foods, this deficiency is seldom seen	No known effects	Liver, eggs, wheat germ, peanuts, and peas; widely distributed in most foods
Biotin	Essential for metabolism of protein, fats, and carbohydrates and energy release	Dermatitis, loss of appetite, nausea, insomnia, deep depression, and muscle pain. Occurs only when large quantities of raw egg whites are consumed over a long period since audin, a protein in raw egg white, blocks absorption of biotin	No known effects	Widely distributed in food, but the best sources are liver, egg yolk, nuts, and legumes
Folic Acid	Essential for the synthesis of nucleic acids, the building blocks life	Smooth red tongue, intestinal distress, macrocytic of anemia and failure of young red blood cells to mature	No known effects	Liver, leafy vegetables, dried beans and peas, asparagus and broccoli, fresh oranges, whole wheat flours, breads, and cereals
B_{12}	Synthesis of nucleic acids and the amino acid, aspartic acid	Sore tongue, weakness, weight loss, tingling hands and feet, back pain, mental and nervous changes, eventually pernicious anemia, and irreversible deterioration of the spinal cord	No known effects	Only in animal foods like liver, meats, poultry, fish, and shellfish, eggs and milk and milk products

Glossary of Dietary Terms

CONTENTS

	Page
Absorption .... Available	1
Avidin ....Carbohydrate	2
Carob powder .... Denaturation	3
Dixtrin ....Exchange list	4
Excipient ....Hyperkalemia	5
Hyperlipoproteinemia ....Lactose intolerance	6
Lecithin ....Mineral oil	7
Monosaccharides ....Pasteurized	8
Pellagra ....Saccharin	9
Salt ....Urea	10
Uremia ....Zinc	11

Glossary of Dietary Terms

Absorption. Assimilation or taking up of nutrients, fluids, gases, or other substances by the stomach or intestinal walls following digestion.

Acetone (dimethyl ketone). Product of incomplete oxidation of fats. May occur in diabetes mellitus, giving a fruity odor to the breath.

Acid-forming foods. Foods in which the acidic residue exceeds the alkaline residue.

Acidosis. An abnormal increase of acids in the blood caused by accumulation of an excess of acids in the body or by excessive loss of base; characterized by a fall in the pH of the blood or decrease in the alkali reserve in the body. Examples of acidosis include the ketosis (of diabetes mellitus), phosphoric, sulfuric, and hydrochloric acids (of renal insufficiency), lactic acid (or prolonged exercise), and carbonic acid (in respiratory disease).

ADA. Abbreviation for the American Dietetic Association, American Diabetes Association, and American Dental Association.

Adipose. Fat or fatty.

Alcohol. Ethanol. Ethyl alcohol. Distilled from the products of anaerobic fermentation of carbohydrate. An ingredient in a variety of beverages including beer, wine, liqueurs, cordials, and mixed or straight drinks. Pure alcohol itself yields about seven Calories per gram, of which more than 75 percent is available to the body.

Alkaline-forming foods. Foods in which the alkaline residue exceeds the acidic residue.

Alkalosis. An excess of base in the body, commonly resulting from persistent vomiting, excessive sodium bicarbonate intake, or hyperventilation. An abnormal condition of elevated blood pH caused by excessive loss of acids from the body without comparable loss of base or more supply of base than can be neutralized or eliminated.

Allergen. Any agent or substance (usually protein) capable of producing an allergic reaction.

Amino acid (AA). Chief components of proteins. Each amino acid molecule contains one or more amino group (— NH_2) and carboxyl group (— COOH). Amino acids may be acid, basic, or neutral.

Anabolism. Process of building simple substances into more complex substances.

Anemia. Deficiency in the circulating hemoglobin, red blood cells, or packed cell volume resulting in decreased capacity of the blood to carry oxygen. Macrocytic (large cell size) anemias may result from folacin and B_{12} deficiencies. Microcytic (small cell size), hypochromic (low color index) anemia may result from iron deficiency. Iron, protein, folic acid, vitamin B_{12}, and vitamin C are the major nutrients essential in blood formation.

Anorexia. Lack or loss of appetite for food.

Antibiotic. A substance that destroys or inhibits the growth of bacteria and other micro-organisms.

Antioxidant. A substance which delays or prevents oxidation.

Antivitamin. A substance which may inactivate or destroy a vitamin.

Anuria. Suppression or absence of urinary excretion.

Apatite. Complex calcium phosphate salt giving strength to bones.

Appetite. Natural desire or craving for food.

Arteriosclerosis. Hardening, thickening, and loss of elasticity of the inner walls of arteries and capillaries.

Artificial sweeteners. See saccharin, sorbitol, mannitol, and cyclamate.

Ascorbic acid. Reduced form of vitamin C; water soluble vitamin; prevents scurvy.

Ash. Mineral residue remaining after burning or oxidizing all organic matter.

As Purchased (AP). The weight of food before removing or trimming inedible parts.

Atherosclerosis. A fatty degeneration of the blood vessels and connective tissue of arterial walls. A kind of arteriosclerosis. The fatty deposits, including cholesterol, phospholipids, triglycerides, and other substances, decrease the internal channel size of the blood vessel.

Atony. Lack of normal tone or strength.

Atrophy. A wasting away of the cell, tissue, or organ.

Available. A nutrient that is in a form readily

absorbed by the digestive tract and usable by the body.

Avidin. A protein in raw egg white which binds with the B vitamin, biotin, and prevents its absorption from the digestive tract. Cooking inactivates avidin.

Avitaminosis. A condition due to inadequate vitamin intake or absorption, increased body require. ment, or antivitamins.

Azotemia uremia. Retention of urea or other nitrogenous substances in the urine.

Balance study. Quantitative method of measuring amount of a nutrient ingested and excreted to determine retention (positive balance) or loss (negative balance).

Basal metabolism. Energy expended at complete physical and mental rest (12-to-16 hours after food ingestion and in thermally neutral temperature). Includes energy for respiration, circulation, gastrointestinal contractions, muscle tone, body temperature, and organ function. Basal metabolic rate (BMR) for an adult is approximately one Calorie per kilogram body weight per hour.

Beikost. Foods other than milk or formula.

Beriberi. Nutritional deficiency of thiamin (vitamin B_1) resulting in loss of appetite, general weakness, progressive edema, polyneuritis, and enlarged heart.

Bile. A fluid produced in the liver, stored, and concentrated in the gallbladder, and emptied into the duodenum to aid in digestion of fat.

Biological value (BV). The efficiency of food protein in supplying amino acids in the proper amounts for protein synthesis in the body. For example, meat has a high biological value (HBV) and beans have a low value. The Thomas-Mitchell equation for calculating BV follows:

$$\%BV = 100\% \times \frac{N\ intake - [(FN-MN) + (UNEN)]}{N\ intake - (FN-MN)}$$

where N = nitrogen, FN = fecal nitrogen, MN = metabolic nitrogen, UN = urinary nitrogen, and EN = endogenous nitrogen.

Biotin. A member of the water-soluble vitamin B complex; aids in fixation of carbon dioxide in fatty acid synthesis. Widely distributed in foodstuffs and synthesized by intestinal bacteria. Deficiency may be induced by large amount of avidin, causing scaly dermatitis, muscle pains, general malaise, and depression.

Bland. Any food that is not irritating to the gastric mucosa.

Blood lipids. Primarily cholesterol, phospholipid, and triglyceride which are bound to protein and circulate in the plasma.

Blood sugar level (BSL). The level of glucose (blood sugar) per 100 ml blood.

Bowel. The intestines.

Bran. The outer layer of whole grain. It contains iron, phosphorus, B vitamins, and fiber. Fiber absorbs water, softens and increases the bulk of stools, and facilitates elimination.

Brat diet. Diet consisting of banana, rice, applesauce, and toast; prescribed for diarrhea, especially for infants and children.

Bulk. The indigestible portion of carbohydrates which cannot he hydrolyzed by gastrointestinal enzymes.

Bulking agent. A metabolically inert substance which increases food volume without increasing calories.

BUN. Blood urea nitrogen.

Caffeine. An alkaloidal purine in coffee, tea, and cola drinks. A cardiac and renal stimulant which produces varying pharmacologic responses.

Calciferol. Vitamin D_2. A fat soluble vitamin produced by ergosterol irradiation. Prevents rickets.

Calcium. A major mineral, essential in bone formation, blood clotting, muscle tone, and nerve function. Deficiency may result in rickets or possibly osteomalacia.

Caffeine. An alkaloidal purine in coffee, tea, and cola drinks. A cardiac and renal stimulant which produces varying pharmacologic responses.

Calciferol. Vitamin D2. A fat soluble vitamin produced by ergosterol irradiation. Prevents rickets.

Calcium. A major mineral, essential in bone formation, blood clotting, muscle tone, and nerve function. Deficiency may result in rickets or possibly osteomalacia.

Calorie. The amount of heat energy required to raise the temperature of one kilogram of water one degree Centigrade. This is the large Calorie, or kilocalorie as used in nutrition. Calories come from carbohydrate, protein, fat, alcohol, and alcohol derivatives (like sorbitol).

Calculus. Commonly called stone.

Carbohydrate. One of three major energy sources in food. Contains carbon, hydrogen, and oxygen. *Available carbohydrates*, such as sugar and starch, provide glucose and glycogen to the body and supply four Calories per gram. *Indigestible carbohydrate* is primarily indigestible plant cellulose.

Carob powder. A powder that looks and tastes like chocolate but does not contain lactose. It may be used as a substitute for chocolate on lactose and galactose restricted diets.

Carotene. Yellow-red plant pigment converted in the body to vitamin A. Two international units of betacarotene are equivalent to one international unit of vitamin A. Abundant in green leafy, and yellow vegetables.

Casein. A milk protein which can contain large amounts of lactose. A phosphoprotein.

Casein hydrolysate. Chemical decomposition of the principal protein of milk.

Catabolism. Opposite of anabolism. Metabolic process in which complex substances are broken down into simpler substances, usually yielding energy. Destructive metabolism.

Catecholamines. Chemicals synthesized in the brain, sympathetic nerve endings, peripheral tissues, and adrenal medulla.

Celiac disease. Malabsorptive syndrome due to sensitivity to gluten and resulting in decreased jejunal mucosa absorption of fat, carbohydrates, protein, vitamins, and minerals. See Wheat Elimination, paragraph 11-3.

Cellulose. The structural fibers in plants. Indigestible polysaccharide which provides bulk to the diet.

Cholecalciferol. Vitamin D_2. Initiates production of a calcium-binding protein.

Cholesterol. Fat-like steroid alcohol found in all tissues. It may be synthesized in the body, but is usually absorbed from the digestive tract in the presence of fat. It is excreted in bile. Foods of animal origin are dietary sources of cholesterol. It is a key part of the fatty deposits in the arterial wall in atherosclerosis.

Choline. A component of lecithin. Necessary for fat transport, preventing accumulation of fat in the liver. Occurs in all plant and animal cells and may be synthesized from glycine (an amino acid) in the presence of a methyl group.

Chylomicron. A blood lipoprotein containing primarily triglycerides from dietary fat and smaller amounts of cholesterol, phospholipid, and protein.

Chyluria. The presence of a fat globule emulsion, formed in the small intestine after digestion, in the urine giving it a milky appearance.

Clinical nutrition. That branch of the health sciences having to do with the diagnosis, treatment, and prevention of human disease caused by deficiency, excess, or metabolic imbalance of dietary nutrients.

Cobalamin. Vitamin B_{12}. Antipernicious anemia factor; extrinsic factor.

Coffee oils. Possible cause of gastrointestinal irritation, diarrhea is a common symptom.

Colloid. A material whose particles are between 1 and 100 millimicrons in size and dispersed throughout a medium. The particles in dispersion are larger than ordinary crystalloid molecules but are not large enough to settle out under the influence of gravity. Examples are blood protein and gelatin.

Connective tissue. Collagen and elastin. Collagen is converted to gelatin by moist heat cookery. Elastin is not broken down or softened in cooking.

Creatinine. One of the end products of food protein breakdown. The amount excreted in the urine is an index of muscle mass and may be used as a measure of basal heat production. **Clear liquid dessert.** Desserts that provide little or no residue, including plain gelatin and Popsicles.

Crystalloid. Small molecules dissolved in a medium such as salt dissolved in water. Other examples are Na^+, K^+, other electrolytes, BUN, uric acid, and creatinine dissolved in the blood.

Curds. The clumped part of curdled milk which contains lactose.

Cyanocobalamin. Vitamin B_{12}.

Cyclamates. A noncaloric sweetener with 30 to 60 times the sweet taste of sucrose. A sodium or calcium salt of cyclohexylsulfamic acid. Cyclamate was changed from the GRAS (generally recognized as safe by the Food and Drug Administration) list to drug status, permitting use only under medical supervision. A suspected carcinogen.

Dehydration. Removal of water from food, tissue, or substrate.

Dehydroascorbic acid. Oxidized vitamin C; biologically active; reversibly oxidized and reduced. **Deciliter.** One-tenth of a liter.

Denaturation. To change the chemical,

physical, or biologic properties of protein by heating, freezing, irradiation, pressure, or organic solvent application.

Dextrin. The intermediate product of starch breakdown; a polysaccharide.

Dialysis. To separate substances in a solution by using a semipermeable membrane; small substances will pass through and larger molecules will not. As used in food preparation, see attachment 5.

Diet. Food and drink consumed. See specific types in text.

Dietary consultation. Individualized professional guidance provided to assist patients in adapting food consumption to meet health needs. The patient's background, socioeconomic needs, and personal preferences are considered when instructing patients on the physician-prescribed diet.

Dietary history. Record of an individual's food intake taken by 24-hour recall or repeated food records. Basis for individualized dietary consultation.

Dietary status. Bodily condition resulting from the utilization of the essential nutrients available to the body. Dietary history provides some indication of dietary status.

Dietetics. The science and art of planning, preparing, and serving meals to individuals and groups according to the principles of nutrition and management; economic, social, cultural, psychological, and health or disease conditions are considered.

Dietitian. A professional who practices dietetics after following a prescribed academic program for a baccalaureate degree in an accredited institution and completing an accredited internship, or equivalent.

Dietitian, Registered (R.D.). A qualified dietitian who has also successfully completed the examination for professional registration and maintains continuing education requirements by completing 75 clock hours of professional education every 5 years.

Digestibility. The amount of nutrient absorbed by the body and not excreted in the feces.

Digestion. Process of converting food into substances which can be absorbed by the body.

Disaccharidase. An enzyme which hydrolyzes disaccharides to yield two single sugars.

Diuresis. Increased secretion of urine.

Dumping syndrome. Postgastrectomy epigastric discomfort resulting when a large amount of hypertonic, concentrated food draws large quantities of fluid from the bloodstream into the intestine.

Duodenum. The first segment of small intestine between the pylorus and jejunum. Pancreatic juice and bile are secreted into the duodenum.

Edible portion (EP). The trimmed weight of food that is normally eaten.

Effusion. Fluid escaping into a part or tissue.

Endogenous. Originating within the cell or tissue.

Endogenous protein. Body or tissue protein.

Energy. Capacity to do work, such as muscular activity, maintaining body temperature, and operating metabolic processes. As obtained from food oxidation, energy is expressed in calories.

Enrichment. The addition of one or more nutrients to a food to attain a higher level of those nutrients than normally present in the food. Bread and flour are often enriched.

Enteral. Within or by way of the intestine. Often used to refer to supplemental oral, or tube feedings.

Enzyme. An organic compound (usually protein) which accelerates metabolic reactions (such as digestion).

Epinephrine. A hormone released primarily in response to hypoglycemia. It increases blood pressure, stimulates the heart muscle, accelerates the heart rate, and increases cardiac output.

Ergosterol. A plant steroid converted to vitamin D_2, calciferol, upon irradiation or exposure to ultraviolet light.

Essential amino acid. Those amino acids that cannot be synthesized by the body; they must be obtained from food to ensure normal growth, development, and tissue repair.

Essential fatty acid. Fatty acids that cannot be synthesized in adequate amounts by the body to ensure growth, reproduction, skin health, and proper fat utilization.

Ethanol. See alcohol.

Ethylenediamine-tetraacetate. A non-nutritive food additive used to separate a part from a whole, or to act as a metal scavenger.

Exchange list. Grouping of foods similar in nutrients together so they may be used interchangeably.

Excipient. Any addition to a medicine designed to permit proper shaping or consistency.

Exogenous. Originating outside, externally caused. Extrinsic factor. Vitamin B_{12}.

Exudative enteropathics. Any disease of the intestine with material escaped from the blood vessels deposited in the intestine.

Fat. One of three major sources of food energy, which provides nine Calories per gram. A mixture of glyceryl esters of fatty acids; an oily, yellow, or white substance of animal or vegetable sources.

Fatty acid. Organic acids which combine with glycerol to form fat.

Favism. An acute hemolytic anemia resulting from ingestion of fava beans (horse or broad beans).

Ferment. Chemical change caused by digestive enzymes of micro-organisms.

Fiber. An indigestible part of fruits, vegetables, cereals, and grains important in the diet as roughage, or bulk.

Flatulence. Excessive gas in the stomach or intestines.

Focacin. Folic acid. Pteroylglutamic acid. A water-soluble vitamin of the B complex group needed for normal growth and hemopoiesis. Widely distributed in plant and animal tissues. Deficiency may be induced by sulfonamides or folic acid antagonists.

Food habit. Usual pattern of an individual or group for choosing, preparing, and eating food resulting from family, cultural, economic, and religious influences.

Fortification. The addition of one or more nutrients to a food whether or not they are naturally present. An example is margarine fortified with vitamin A.

Full liquid dessert. Desserts that are fluid or that easily become fluid, including plain gelatin, ice cream, soft custard, and pudding.

Galactose. A six carbon monosaccharide.

Galactosemia. Galactose in the blood due to an inborn error of metabolism in which the enzyme galactose-l-phosphate uridyl transferase is absent; thus, galactose is not converted to glucose. Mental and growth retardation, liver and spleen enlargement, cataracts, jaundice, weight loss, vomiting, and diarrhea result unless dietary modification eliminates lactose-and galactose-containing foods from the diet.

Gavage. Feeding via insertion of a tube through the mouth into the stomach.

Gelatin. An incomplete protein obtained from partial hydrolysis of collagen.

Geriatrics. Study and treatment of diseases and problems occurring in old age.

Glomerular filtration rate (GFR). Milliliters of blood which pass through the kidney glomeruli in one minute; may be used to estimate kidney function.

Glucose. Dextrose. Grape sugar. Blood sugar. A monosaccharide which may be absorbed into the bloodstream and is the major source of energy for the brain and nervous tissues.

Glutathione. A tripeptide believed to assist sulfhydryl containing enzymes to stay in the reduced state essential for their activity.

Gluten. A cereal grain protein; gluten provides elasticity to bread dough.

Glycogen. A polysaccharide composed of glucose units. The main form of carbohydrate stored by man and animals in liver, muscles, and other tissues.

Gram. A unit of mass and weight in the metric system. An ounce is approximately 28 grams.

Gravidity. Pregnancy.

Hemicellulose. A largely indigestible plant polysaccharide that absorbs water. Pectin is a hemi-cellulose that may lower serum cholesterol.

Hemodialysis. Dialyzing blood to remove waste products.

Hepatosplenomegaly. Enlargement of both liver and spleen.

High biological value (HBV) protein. A protein readily digested, absorbed, and utilized by the body, such as the protein in eggs.

Homeostasis. Balance of the internal environment including fluid, pH, body temperature, blood sugar level, heart and pulse rates, and hormonal control.

Hydrogenated oil. Addition of molecular hydrogen to double bonds in unsaturated fatty acids creating saturated solid fat with reduced essential fatty acid biological value.

Hypercholesterolemia. Elevated blood cholesterol associated with cardiovascular diseases.

Hyperchylomicronemia. Elevation of chylomicron lipoproteins circulating in the blood.

Hyperkalemia. Increased potassium in the blood. Hyperlipidemia. An elevation of one or

more lipid constituents of the blood.
Hyperlipoproteinemia. Elevation of blood lipoproteins.
Hypernatremia. Excessive amount of sodium in the blood.
Idiopathic. Without known origin.
Ileum. The part of the small intestine between the jejunum and large intestine.
Inborn error of metabolism. A metabolic defect existing at birth due to missing genes.
Incomplete protein. A protein lacking one or more essential amino acids.
Ingestion. Eating or drinking; taking in.
Inorganic. Minerals that do not contain carbon.
Inositol. A water soluble alcohol found primarily in cereal grains which combines with phosphate to form phytic acid.
Instant cereal. Pregelatinized (precooked) cereal requiring addition of water before serving.
Insulin. A hormone secreted by the beta cells of the islets of Langerhans in the pancreas. It is essential to carbohydrate metabolism in the body. Exogenous insulin is injected by some diabetics to provide proper carbohydrate metabolism.
Insulin shock (or) reaction. Very low blood sugar level resulting from overdose of insulin. Symptoms include hunger, weakness, nervousness, double vision, shallow breathing, sweating, headache, dizziness, mental confusion, muscular twitching, convulsion, loss of consciousness, coma, and eventually death. Fruit juice or intravenous glucose are often used to counteract insulin reaction.
International unit. A measure of biologic activity of a nutrient.
Interpolate. To determine intermediate values in a series based on observed values or to introduce new material in a given subject.
Intrinsic factor. Chemical in gastric juice that facilitates vitamin B_{12} (extrinsic factor) absorption. Lack of intrinsic factor results in pernicious anemia.
Iodine. A trace mineral essential in regulating basal metabolism. Deficiency results in goiter.
Iodine number (or) value. The number of grams of iodine absorbed by 100 grams of fat. Indicates the amount of fatty acids and degree of unsaturation of a fat. The iodine number of saturated coconut oil is 10, and that of polyunsaturated safflower oil is 100.

Iodized salt. Table salt with one part sodium or potassium iodide per 5,000 to 10,000 parts sodium chloride.
Irradiation. Exposure to ultraviolet rays used for destroying microorganisms in food and converting provitamin D to active vitamin D.
Isocaloric. Containing an equal number of Calories.
Jejunum. The part of the small intestine between the duodenum and ileum.
Joule. A metric measure of energy equaling 4.184 Calories.
Junket. The precipitated protein of milk casein and fat.
Ketogenic-antiketogenic ratio. The ratio of the amount of ketogenic factors, such as fatty acids and ketogenic amino acids, to the amount of anti-ketogenic factors, such as carbohydrates, glucogenic amino acids, and the glycerol of fat.
Ketosis. An accumulation of ketone bodies (beta-hydroxybutyric acid, acetoacetic acid, and acetone) from incomplete fatty acid oxidation. Uncontrolled ketosis may result in acidosis.
Kosher foods. Foods prepared and served by Orthodox Judaism dietary laws which include: (1) milk and meat are not consumed at the same meal, (2) meat must be slaughtered in a special ordained manner and cleaned (koshered) by soaking in water, salting, and washing, (3) meat from cud-chewing, cloven-hooved animals (cows, sheep, goats) may be eaten, (4) finfish may be eaten. No pork or shellfish are eaten.
Kwashiorkor. Severe protein malnutrition in children resulting in retarded growth, anemia, edema, fatty liver, lack of pigment in the hair and skin, gastrointestinal disorders, muscle atrophy, and psychomotor wasting.
Labile. Unstable.
Lactase. Enzyme that splits lactose to glucose and galactose.
Lactate, lactic acid, lactalbumin. Substances related to lactose but which cannot be changed into galactose by the body.
Lacto-ovo-vegetarian. Person subsisting on grains, legumes, vegetables, fruits, milk, and eggs. Meat, poultry and fish are avoided.
Lactose. "Milk sugar." Disaccharide occurring in milk products. Contains one glucose and one galactose group.
Lactose intolerance. Lactose malabsorption due to lactase deficiency. Results in

diarrhea.

Lecithin. Phosphatidyl choline. A phospholipid containing glycerol, fatty acids, phosphoric acid, and choline. Involved in fat transport, lecithin is found in many cells, especially nerves. Lecithin synthesis in the body depends upon dietary intake of methyl groups or choline.

Leucine. An essential amino acid with ketogenic properties.

Licorice. Black flavoring extract containing glycyrrhizic acid which, in large amounts, can cause hypertension and hypokalemia.

Lignin. A constituent of crude fiber. An indigestible cellulose. With cellulose, the principal Part of the woody plants. Unlike cellulose, lignin can combine with bile to form insoluble complexes which are not absorbed.

Linoleic acid. Polyunsaturated essential fatty acid with 18 carbon atoms and two double bonds.

Linolenic acid. A nonessential polyunsaturated fatty acid with 18 carbon atoms and three double bonds.

Lipid. Fat or fat-like substances. Includes fatty acids, triglycerides, phosphatides (such as lecithin), terpenes, and steroids (such as cholesterol).

Lipoprotein. A compound consisting of a simple protein and lipid and involved in lipid transport. Types of lipoprotein circulating in the blood include chylomicrons, alpha lipoproteins (high density lipoproteins, HDL), prebeta lipoproteins (very low density lipoproteins, VLDL), and beta lipoprotein (low density lipoprotein, LDL). All are composed of phospholipid, triglyceride, cholesterol, and protein.

Long-chain fatty acid. Fatty acids containing 12 or more carbon atoms, such as stearic (18 carbon) and palmatic (16 carbon) acids.

Low sodium milk. Milk processed by ion-exchange process to remove approximately 90 percent of the naturally occurring sodium. Thiamin, riboflavin, and calcium are also decreased with an increase in potassium.

Lycine. An essential amino acid and the limiting amino acid in many cereal products.

Magnesium. An essential mineral. A cofactor in metabolism.

Malabsorption syndrome. A condition caused by failure of the body to absorb nutrients such as fats, calcium and other minerals, and vitamins. Examples include celiac disease, chronic pancrea-titis, sprue, cystic fibrosis, and carbohydrate intolerance.

Malnutrition. Lack or excess of absorbed nutrients resulting in impaired health status.

Manganese. An essential trace mineral.

Mannitol. A partially absorbed sugar alcohol with a sweet taste equal to sugar but with half the calories.

Maple syrup urine disease. Inborn error of metabolism treated with dietary restriction of leucine. isoleucine, and valine.

Marasmus. Severe protein-calorie malnutrition of infants and young children.

Medium chain fatty acid. Fatty acids containing 8 to 10 carbon atoms, such as caprylic (8 carbon) and capric (10 carbon) acids.

Medium chain triglyceride (MCT). A fat composed primarily of saturated fatty acids with 8 to 10 carbon atoms. A commercially prepared food product for persons not able to digest or absorb food fats and oils.

Menadione. A synthetic, vitamin K_2 is much more potent biologically than vitamin K.

Metabolism. Chemical changes in the body: anabolism and catabolism.

Methionine. An essential amino acid important in protein and fat, metabolism.

Methylcellulose. Indigestible polysaccharide which provides bulk and satiety without. calories.

Micronutrient. Nutrients present. in less than 0.005 percent of body weight, such as trace minerals. Also, nutrients present in very small amounts in food.

Microgram. A metric system unit of mass representing one one-millionth of a gram or one one-thousandth of a milligram.

Milk-alkali syndrome. Ingestion of large quantities of milk and alkalies resulting in hypercalcemia, calcium in soft tissues, vomiting, gastrointestinal bleeding, and high blood pressure.

Milliosmole. One thousandth of an osmole.

Mineral. Inorganic elements that build and repair body tissue or control body functions. The ones known to be essential to man are calcium, chlorine, chromium, cobalt, copper, fluorine, iodine, iron, magnesium, manganese, molybdenum, phosphorus, potassium, selenium, sodium, sulfur. and zinc.

Mineral oil. Liquid petroleum substance which is not absorbed by the gastrointestinal tract but interferes with absorption of fat soluble vitamins.

Monosaccharides. Carbohydrates composed of single simple sugars that cannot be hydrolyzed (broken) into smaller units. Examples are fructose, galactose, glucose, and ribose.

Monounsaturated fat. Fat that neither raises nor lowers blood cholesterol. Examples are olive oil and peanut oil.

Monounsaturated fatty acid. Fatty acids with only one unsaturated double bond.

Monosodium glutamate (MSG). A sodium-containing flavoring used in Asian cookery.

Nasogastric tube. Used in tube feeding; a tube inserted via the nose and esophagus into the stomach.

Nausea. Stomach discomfort with a tendency to vomit.

Negative nitrogen balance. Daily nitrogen excretion greater than nitrogen intake which may be brought about by fever, surgery, or burns.

Niacin. Nicotenic acid. A water-soluble B complex vitamin. Antipellagra factor. Necessary to cell respiration, carbohydrate and protein metabolism, and lipid synthesis; thus, requirement varies with caloric intake.

Niacin equivalent. The sum of nicotinic acid and niacin is the niacin equivalent. Sixty milligrams tryptophan may be converted to one milligram nicotinic acid.

Nicotinic acid. Niacin.

Nitrogen balance/equilibrium. An individual is in nitrogen balance when the nitrogen intake from food protein each day is approximately equal to the nitrogen loss in feces and urine.

Non-nutritive sweetener. A noncaloric synthetic sugar substitute. Examples are saccharine and cyclamate.

Norepinephrine. A hormone released primarily in response to hypotension to raise blood pressure.

Nutrient. Any chemical substance useful in nutrition for providing heat and energy, building and repairing tissues, and regulating life processes.

Nutrition. The study of food in relation to health. Combination of processes by which the body receives and uses the materials necessary for body functions, energy, growth, and tissue renewal.

Nutrition history. Laboratory and clinical findings, and a dietary history.

Nutritional status. The condition of the body resulting from consumption and utilization of nutrients.

Nutriture. Tissue nutrient balance of supply and demand.

Obesity. Fat. Body weight approximately 20 percent or more above desirable weight due to adiposity.

Oil. A lipid that is liquid at room temperature.

Oleic acid. An 18 carbon monounsaturated fatty acid abundant in fats and oils.

Oliguria. Decreased urinary output in relation to fluid intake.

Oral hypoglycemic agents. Orally administered compounds that stimulate beta cells in the islands of Langerhans of the pancreas to secrete endogenous insulin that reduces blood glucose in diabetics. Contraindicated for some patients.

Osmolality. A property of a solution which depends on the concentration of the solute per unit of solvent.

Osmolarity. A property of a solution which depends on the concentration of the solute per unit of total volume of solution.

Osmole. The standard unit of osmotic pressure. Overweight. Fat. Body weight approximately 10 to 20 percent above desirable weight due to adiposity.

Oxalate. Salt of oxalic acid. When combined in insoluble calcium salts. oxalate renders calcium unavailable for absorption.

Pancreatic juice. A digestive juice produced by the pancreas and secreted into the duodenum; contains enzymes involved in digestion of protein, carbohydrate. and fat.

Pantothenic acid. A water-soluble B complex vitamin that is part of coenzyme A. It is essential for growth. normal skin. nervous system development, and adrenal cortex function.

Papain. A proteolytic enzyme of papaya often used as a meat tenderizer.

Parenteral feeding. Food provided without use of the mouth and digestive tract, such as intravenous feeding.

Pasteurized. Heat treated to kill most pathogenic microorganisms. For example. pasteurized eggnog prevents the potential of salmonella infection from eggnog made with raw eggs.

Pellagra. Multiple B vitamin deficiency, notably

of niacin. Symptoms include dermatitis, diarrhea, dementia, and death.

Peristalsis. Alternate contraction and relaxation pf the gastrointestinal tract which moves contents toward the anus.

Pernicious anemia. Chronic macrocytic anemia due to B_{12} and intrinsic factor deficiency.

pH. A measure of acidity and alkalinity.

Phenylalanine. An essential amino that may be converted to tyrosine. It can be ketogenic, glycogenic, and participate in transamination.

Phenylketonuria (PKU). Inborn error in metabolism resulting in the lack of the enzyme phenylal-anine hydroxylase. Phenylalanine cannot be converted to tyrosine without this enzyme. The resultant high levels of phenylalanine result in permanent mental retardation and poor growth and development unless there is close dietary control of phenylalanine ingestion.

Phosphorus. An essential mineral.

Polysaccharide. A complex carbohydrate containing more than four monosaccharides. Examples are glycogen, starch, and cellulose.

Polyunsaturated fatty acids (PUFA). Fatty acids with more than one unsaturated bond in the molecule.

Polyunsaturated: saturated fatty acid ratio (P/S ratio). The relative amount of polyunsaturated linoleic acid to total saturated fatty acids.

Positive nitrogen balance. Nitrogen intake exceeds nitrogen output, such as during infancy and childhood (tissue anabolism).

Potassium. An essential mineral of the intracellular fluids.

Pressor agent. Any substance that raises blood pressure.

Protein. The primary structure of plant and animal bodies. It is composed of amino acids and is approximately 16 percent nitrogen. Protein provides four Calories per gram.

Protein hydrolysate. A mixture of "predigested protein" in the form of amino acids and polypep-tides. Used for oral or parenteral feeding in cases of impaired digestion, such as pancreatic diseases.

Protein calorie malnutrition. A condition of severe tissue wasting, subcutaneous fat loss, and dehydration caused by inadequate protein and calorie intake.

Protein quality. A complete protein contains all the essential amino acids for growth and life. A partial protein maintains life but not growth. An incomplete protein can support neither growth nor life. If two incomplete proteins each supply the limiting amino acid(s) of the other, together they may be capable of supporting growth and life.

Protein-sparing. Refers to calories supplied by carbohydrates and fat. These calories save protein from being "burned" as energy so it may be used for anabolism.

Provitamin. A substance related to a vitamin but with no vitamin activity until it is converted to the biologically active form.

P/S ratio. Ratio of polyunsaturated to saturated fatty acids.

Pureed. A food blenderized to a paste consistency. Most baby foods are pureed.

Purine. Nitrogenous compounds of dietary or endogenous origin catabolized to uric acid in the body.

Pyridoxine. An alcohol form of vitamin 136, a B complex vitamin.

Quick-cooking cereal/rice. Cereals and rice that have disodium phosphate added to reduce their preparation time.

Raffinose. Trisaccharide containing glucose, galactose, and fructose. It is found in beets, roots, underground stems, cottonseed meal, and molasses.

Recommended (Daily) Dietary Allowances (RDA). Suggested amounts of nutrients to provide when planning diets. Designed to maintain good nutrition in healthy persons of average build and activity in a temperature climate with a margin of safety 10 to 50 percent above normal dietary requirements.

Reconstitute. To restore to the normal state, usually by adding water.

Refuse. Inedible, discarded foodstuffs.

Residue. Amount of bulk remaining in the digestive tract after digestion and absorption.

Retinol. A vitamin A alcohol.

Retinol equivalent (RE). Unit expressing vitamin A activity. One RE = 1 u retinol, 6 u beta-carotene, and 12 u for other provitamin A carotenoids.

Riboflavin. Vitamin B_2. Heat stable, water soluble vitamin essential to the health of skin and eyes.

Rickets. Vitamin D deficiency or disturbance of calcium-phosphorus metabolism.

Saccharin. A noncaloric artificial sweetener 700 times sweeter than sugar.

Salt. Table salt; sodium chloride; NaCl.
Satiety. Sense of fullness or comfort; gratification of appetite.
Saturated fat. A fat with no double bonds; chemically satisfied. Often solid at room temperature and usually of animal origin. Examples are butter, lard, and steak fat.
Scurvy. Vitamin C deficiency disease resulting in swollen bleeding gums, hemorrhage of the skin and mucous membranes, and anemia.
Secretagogue. An agent that stimulates secretion.
Short-chain fatty acid. Those containing four to six carbon atoms, such as caproic (6 carbon) and butyric (4 carbon) acids. Yields only about 5 Calories per gram.
Skinfold measurement. Measurement of the thickness of skin at body sites where adipose is normally deposited. Measured with a caliper and compared against a standard chart, it provides an estimate of degree of fatness.
Sodium. An essential mineral important in extra-cellular body fluids and in regulating many body functions.
Soft. Any easily digested food that is soft in texture and provides no harsh fibers or connective tissue.
Sorbitol. A sugar alcohol apparently metabolized without insulin. It contains 4 calories per gram and can be converted to utilizable carbohydrate in the form of glucose. Excessive use may cause gastrointestinal discomfort and diarrhea.
Specific dynamic action. Increased metabolism from heat of digesting, absorbing, and metabolizing food. Approximately 30 percent for protein, 13 percent, for fat, and 4 to 5 percent for carbohydrate.
Standard of identity of foods. Standards established by a government agency, primarily the US Food and Drug Administration, to define quality and container fill for foods.
Stachyose. Tetrasaccharide containing glucose, fructose, and two molecules of galactose. It is found in tubers, peas, lima beans, and beets.
Starch. Plant storage form of carbohydrate (just as the animal storage form is glycogen). A complex polysaccharide. Food sources include breads, cereals, and starchy vegetables.

Sucrose. Table sugar. A disaccharide composed of glucose and fructose.
Sugar. Sucrose. A sweet, soluble carbohydrate that provides 4 Calories of energy per gram.
Sulphur. An essential mineral.
Supplement. A concentrated source of nutrients, such as vitamins or minerals.
Supplementary feeding. Food provided in addition to regular meals to increase nutrient intake.
Sweetening agent (or) sweeteners. Natural sweeteners, such as sugar, or synthetic sweeteners, such as saccharin.
Synthesis. Putting elements together to form a whole.
Tea tannin. Possible cause of constipation.
Textured vegetable protein. Vegetable protein that is flavored, colored, and textured to resemble meat and poultry products.
Theobromine. The alkaloidal stimulant in cocoa beans, tea leaves, and cola nuts that acts as a diuretic, arterial dilator, and myocardial stimulant.
Thiamin. Vitamin B_2, a B complex vitamin and part of a coenzyme important in carbohydrate metabolism. Prevents beriberi.
Threonine. An essential amino acid.
Tocopherols. An alcohol-like group of substances. Four forms have vitamin E activity.
Tofu. Soybean curd; usually available in oriental grocery stores.
Trace minerals. Minerals required by the body in minute amounts.
Triglyceride. A fat composed of a glycerol molecule with three fatty acids.
Tryptophane. An essential amino acid. May be converted to niacin, and a source of the vasoconstrictor serotonin.
Tyramine. A decarboxylation product of tyrosine found in fermented cheeses, wines, and other foods. Produces severe hypertensive reaction if consumed in conjunction with monoamine oxidase inhibitory drugs.
Underweight. Body weight 10 percent or more below the established standards.
Unsaturated fatty acids. Those with one or more double bonds. Abundant in vegetable oils.
Urea. Major nitrogen containing product of protein metabolism and chief nitrogenous constituent of the urine.

Uremia. A toxic condition caused by the retention in the blood of urinary constituents including urea, creatine, uric acid, and other end products of protein metabolism.

Vasopressor. Any agent that causes contraction of the muscular tissue lining the arteries and capillaries.

Vegetarian (or) vegan. Person subsisting entirely or in a large part on fruits, grains, legumes, and vegetables. If eggs, fish, meat, milk, and poultry are totally excluded, a vegetarian diet may be deficient in calcium, phosphorus, riboflavin, and vitamins B_{12} and D. Pure vegetarian diets are usually inadequate in protein for children.

Viosterol. Vitamin D_2, a product of ergosterol irradiation.

Vitamin. Organic substance provided in minute amounts in food or endogenuously synthesized. Essential in metabolic functions.

Vitamin A. Fat-soluble vitamin necessary for normal skin and bone development, maintenance of vision, and synthesis of mucopolysaccarides.

Vitamin B complex. Water soluble vitamins often found together in nature. Vitamins B_1 (thiamin), B_2 (riboflavin), B_6 group (pyridoxine, pyridoxal, and pyridoxamine), B_{12} group (cobalamins), nicotinic acid (niacin), pteroylglutamic acid (PGA, folacin, or folic acid), pantothenic acid, and biotin. All except B_{12} are coenzymes.

Vitamin C. Water-soluble vitamin. Ascorbic acid.

Vitamin D. Fat-soluble vitamins including ergocalciferol (D_2) and cholecalciferol (D_3).

Vitamin E. Fat-soluble vitamin. Tocopherols.

Vitamin K. Fat-soluble vitamin consumed in food and produced endogenously by intestinal flora. Necessary for blood clotting.

Water. A major nutrient required by the body. Endogenous water is provided as a byproduct of metabolism. Exogenous water may be in the fluid form or contained in food.

Water requirement. Water functions by removing body heat and urinary excreta. One milliliter water per calorie is usually sufficient unless there is a pathological condition such as fever or burn.

Whey. A clear, watery liquid remaining when milk curdles. It contains lactose, but little or no fat.

Zanthine. Weakly basic alkaloid chemicals including caffeine, theophylline, and theobromine.

Zinc. An essential trace mineral involved in growth, digestion, and metabolism. Deficiency results in retarded growth, delayed sexual maturity, and delayed wound healing.

CPSIA information can be obtained
at www.ICGtesting.com
Printed in the USA
LVHW062103180619
621611LV00010B/477/P

3 1333 04853 7961

9 781731 830050